Performance in a Pandemic

This edited collection gathers UK and international artists, academics, practitioners, and researchers in the fields of contemporary performance, dance, and live art to offer creative-critical responses to the impact of the COVID-19 pandemic on their work.

Themes addressed in these case studies include the ways in which liveness functions across digital platforms, the new demands on audiences and performance-makers, and the impact on international festivals as the digital removes geographical and locational restrictions. Brought together, these examples capture the creative activity and output that this unexpected cultural moment has provoked. Creative-critical responses interrogate what the global pandemic has taught us about what it is to make live work during lockdown and explore what the future of performance-making in a post-COVID world might look like.

For all scholars and performance-makers whose work brings them into the sphere of contemporary art and culture, this is an essential and stimulating account of practice at the beginning of the 2020s.

Laura Bissell is Interim Head of Contemporary Performance Practice and Lecturer in Research at the Royal Conservatoire of Scotland.

Lucy Weir is Chancellor's Fellow in History of Art at the University of Edinburgh, where she specialises in dance and performance studies.

Performance in a Pandemic

Edited by
Laura Bissell and
Lucy Weir

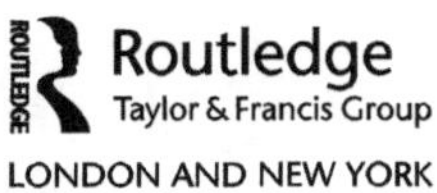

LONDON AND NEW YORK

First published 2022
by Routledge
2 Park Square, Milton Park, Abingdon, Oxon OX14 4RN

and by Routledge
605 Third Avenue, New York, NY 10158

Routledge is an imprint of the Taylor & Francis Group, an informa business

© 2022 selection and editorial matter, Laura Bissell and Lucy Weir; individual chapters, the contributors

The right of Laura Bissell and Lucy Weir to be identified as the authors of the editorial material, and of the authors for their individual chapters, has been asserted in accordance with sections 77 and 78 of the Copyright, Designs and Patents Act 1988.

All rights reserved. No part of this book may be reprinted or reproduced or utilised in any form or by any electronic, mechanical, or other means, now known or hereafter invented, including photocopying and recording, or in any information storage or retrieval system, without permission in writing from the publishers.

Trademark notice: Product or corporate names may be trademarks or registered trademarks, and are used only for identification and explanation without intent to infringe.

British Library Cataloguing-in-Publication Data
A catalogue record for this book is available from the British Library

Library of Congress Cataloging-in-Publication Data
A catalog record has been requested for this book

ISBN: 978-0-367-76134-9 (hbk)
ISBN: 978-1-032-19143-0 (pbk)
ISBN: 978-1-003-16564-4 (ebk)

DOI: 10.4324/9781003165644

Typeset in Times New Roman
by codeMantra

Contents

Contributors

Sarah Bartley

Laura Bissell

Judit Bodor

Rachel Clive

Kate Craddock

Chris Elsden, Diwen Yu, Benedetta Piccio, Ingi Helgason, Melissa Terras

Tamsin Hong

Shona Macnaughton

Judd Morrissey and Mark Jeffery (ATOM-r) in collaboration with **Abraham Avnisan**

Katherine Nolan

Denise Espírito Santo and David Gutiérrez Castañeda

Gudrun Soley Sigurdardottir

Marc Silberschatz

Rebecca Stancliffe

Lito Tsitsou

Lucy Weir

Introducing Performance in a Pandemic

Laura Bissell and Lucy Weir

The COVID-19 pandemic that emerged in early 2020 disrupted the lives of billions of people across the globe. As governments stipulated periods of lockdown to halt the spread of the virus, the rhythms of working, social, and family life came to a jarring halt. In the UK, as in many countries internationally, businesses and institutions were shuttered, schools and childcare facilities closed, and communal gathering not simply discouraged, but prohibited by law. Uncertainty over transmission routes for the virus led to the imposition of social distancing measures – reminders appeared on supermarket floors and throughout public spaces to maintain a safe range of two metres from others inhabiting the same space.

For those who work with or upon the body, this abrupt regulatory change had a devastating effect. The global health crisis and resulting periods of quarantine have dramatically impacted the landscape of performance-making. From March 2020, it was neither possible nor permissible to create live work in the usual ways – theatres and venues were closed, audiences could not gather, and performers could no longer touch, lift, or hold one another. With these new, extensive restrictions inhibiting traditional, in-person creative processes, many artists and makers moved their practices online, creating digital performances and artworks. Meanwhile, others without access to stages, live audiences or, perhaps most crucially, financial support stopped making work altogether. As the crisis ground on, with no imminent end in sight, questions about the viability of performance became more urgent. What would happen to artforms that, until now, have been premised on the presence of live performers and audiences sharing (frequently intimate) space together?

Peggy Phelan and Philip Auslander debated whether live performance is a fleeting, once-in-a-moment experience, where 'its only life is in the present' (Phelan, 1999), or if mediatisation can also be considered

DOI: 10.4324/9781003165644-1

a part of the live. Auslander's claim that 'live forms have become mediatized' (2008) has, surely, been realised throughout the lockdown period and the resultant shift towards online performance practice. He also argues that we can appreciate a performance as live without being in the same place, that 'the power of liveness is in fact a function not of proximity, but distance' (2016: 296). In the context of a global health crisis, Phelan's concept of performance being 'of the moment' moves away from having temporal significance and can instead be considered literally. The performances being developed over digital platforms during lockdown are of the moment – in fact, they are distinctively and uniquely of this moment. The context of quarantine and self-isolation demanded that performance change, in some ways quite radically, in order to exist.

Inspired by these seismic changes in the landscape of performance practice, we felt an urgent need to form a record of this unpredictable, precarious moment for the sector. We circulated an open call for contributions, inviting artists, programmers, and curators to share their perspectives on the most compelling questions around performance practice in the wake of COVID-19. The result, *Performance in a Pandemic*, is a collection of essays, reflections, and creative interventions that centres on a diverse range of professional and personal experiences in the wake of the first government-mandated lockdown in the United Kingdom (March–September 2020). In soliciting these contributions, it was our intention to capture, analyse, and disseminate digital creative output in Scotland, the wider UK, and across the world during the first wave of this crisis. At the same time, we sought to address some of the key questions around liveness, audiences, economy, and precarity within the performing arts that the pandemic has so viscerally exposed.

Perhaps predictably, our call for contributions resulted in a wave of diverse proposals from across the UK and internationally. Despite the broad range of subject matter, key themes recurred time and again. Having invited proposals from artists and performers personally and profoundly impacted by the pandemic, it is unsurprising that one of the first categories we identified centred around grief, lost opportunities, and fears for an uncertain future. Related to this was an overlapping set of concerns around the precarious conditions of creative practice during the pandemic – financial uncertainty and instability now elevated to an even more urgent state of crisis wrought by difficulties accessing government support, but which nonetheless hearkened back to existing and enduring anxieties over funding for the arts. Our proposal explicitly called for contributions from marginalised communities, and, in response, it was heartening to hear of the breadth of initiatives organised by and targeted towards groups who are so often excluded from creative spaces and conversations alike. Finally, the question of preservation arose repeatedly, on the level of both individual and institutional practice, and often intersecting with the omnipresent issue of digital life and online performance. In response, proposals returned time and again to the overarching narratives of care, mutual support, and the importance of community. Collaboration, too, is central – this book is a cooperative effort in itself, but our contributors also explore various methods of collaboration, from interdisciplinary research methods to cross-sector creative and charitable partnerships.

It is perhaps no surprise that the individual pieces that comprise this volume also function in conversation with one another: Kate Craddock writes about fellow author Gudrun Soley Sigurdardottir's performance *Elision* at the Gateshead International Festival of Theatre (GIFT) 2020, for example. Both Sigurdardottir and Sarah Bartley explore creative practice in the criminal justice system and working collaboratively with incarcerated young people and women respectively. These contributions, stylistically distinct from one another, strikingly demonstrate how participatory work within contexts of incarceration continued to find ways of connecting and collaborating with prison populations. Meanwhile, Chris Elsden, Diwen Yu, Benedetta Piccio, Ingi Helgason and Melissa Terras (writing collaboratively) and Kate Craddock talk about the impact of the pandemic upon major arts festivals. Elsden et al focus on the Edinburgh Fringe, capturing the devastation and difficulty of shifting to recorded mediums for many live artists, while Craddock's discussion originates from a more personal perspective, charting how the ethos of GIFT and her previous digital experience helped to shape an exciting, experimental shift towards a digital festival. The theme of precarity is interwoven throughout the book, from Denise Espírito Santo and David Gutiérrez Castañeda's impassioned critique of the impact of COVID-19 on Latin American communities and indigenous populations, to Tamsin Hong's discussion of a cancelled Tate exhibition – her evocative recollection of capturing a single live performance of Faustin Linyekula's work in a near-empty Tanks voices the precarity that the peoples of Central Africa have lived with for centuries. In this respect, our contributors speak to the ways in which COVID-19's repercussions have been experienced more harshly by specific communities. While we have seemingly been weathering the same storm as a global community, in reality, we have not been in the same boat, and the pandemic has further exacerbated existing inequalities and injustices.

The first section of this volume includes a diverse range of responses that focus on **Precarity and Vulnerability**; indeed, this comprised one of the most recurring themes that our call evoked. Here, authors explore a range of experiences around fragility, anxiety, and instability throughout the initial lockdown period. This ranges from the deeply personal to broader, sector-wide considerations: Katherine Nolan explores her role as mother, grieving daughter, and performance artist in the first months of the pandemic, while Lito Tsitsou's chapter maps the impact of COVID-19 on freelance contemporary dancers' and choreographers' work in Scotland and wider national context. Denise Espírito Santo and David Gutiérrez Castañeda's 'Embrace your vulnerability: Cultivating the arts, theatricalities, performativities in times of catastrophe' discusses how some indigenous communities have experienced the pandemic. This section concludes with Judd Morrissey and Mark Jeffery (ATOM-r) in collaboration with Abraham Avnisan, sharing reflections on their work, *The Tenders,* a site-specific yet nonetheless global mixed-reality performance.

The title of the second section, **Art in an emergency: 'It's work'**, is drawn from Olivia Laing's book *Funny Weather: Art in an Emergency,* where she asks if art can do anything in periods of crisis and responds: 'It's work. What art does is provide material with which to think: new registers, new spaces. After that, friend, it is up to you' (2020: 2). Building on the first section's focus on precarity, here our authors examine the 'work' of performance-making in times of crisis. Artist Shona Macnaughton explores her transition to alternative 'gig work', attempting to become a Deliveroo driver when her performance-making work was cancelled. Marc Silberschatz writes from the perspective of a director moving to other modes of performance, and Chris Elsden, Diwen Yu, Benedetta Piccio, Ingi Helgason, and Melissa Terras analyse the shift from live to digital that artists embarked on when the Edinburgh Fringe Festival was unable to take place in August 2020.

The third section, **Outreach and Inclusion**, explores how marginalised and excluded groups were impacted throughout lockdown and how the ethics of participation were reimagined for online spaces. Sarah Bartley's conversation with Anna Herrmann centres on the experiences of incarcerated women during the pandemic, focusing on the issue of increased social isolation – this is a theme continued in Rebecca Stancliffe's chapter, which reflects on creative outreach programmes for older populations during the initial lockdown period. Artist Gudrun Soley Sigurdardottir offers us an invitation, drawing on her experience of working with young people in the criminal justice system throughout this time of enforced distancing, and Rachel Clive brings this section to a close with her account of collaborative, in-person performance-making.

The final section, **Curation: Performing the Archive**, features a range of authors discussing how curatorial practices adapted to the global pandemic and the ways in which the cultural, economic, and artistic impact of COVID-19 has been felt across the sector. Tamsin Hong offers an intimate account of the last-minute cancellation of a live exhibition and provides a striking glimpse into the processes of documenting work in the hours before lockdown came into force in the UK. Judit Bodor focuses on the work of an individual artist, Alastair MacLennan, discussing the curatorial processes and decisions around exhibiting his work made during lockdown. Finally, Kate Craddock's contribution takes a similarly personal approach, exploring her recent experience of transferring the GIFT Festival to an online format, against a backdrop of her prior experience making and sharing art remotely.

What the pandemic has revealed is the often-invisible interconnectedness of disparate people and communities around the world. The intrinsic connectedness of everyone's lives has been harshly exposed, illustrated by the way the virus has spread from country to continent, with no concern for borders, or boundaries. The interconnectedness that our contributors are responding to is also evident in their own synergies and resonances, a tentacular series of reflections on the initial months of the pandemic, and how live art forms, performance, contemporary theatre, dance, and live art began to evolve in response to the restrictions.

This book offers a snapshot of performance work that took place during the first UK lockdown – specifically, from March to September 2020. Crucially, we wish to impress that our collection is not designed to be a comprehensive or complete account of pandemic performance, an undertaking that would require extensive and exhaustive documentation of work that took place online, across social media, outdoors, or in empty theatres. Instead, *Performance in a Pandemic* aims to capture a sense of immediacy, recording the experiences of artists, curators, and academics responding, sometimes in real time, to extraordinary new circumstances. From the announcement of the first stay-at-home order on 23 March 2020, life in the UK changed in an instant. *Performance in a Pandemic* thus captures fragments of activity across a period of rapid change and profound uncertainty.

References

Auslander, P. (2008). *Liveness: Performance in a Mediatized Culture*. London: Routledge.

Auslander, P. (2016). So Close and Yet So Far Away: The Proxemics of Liveness. In: M. Reason and A. M. Lindelof, eds., *Experiencing Liveness in Contemporary Performance: Interdisciplinary Perspectives*. London: Routledge. pp. 295–298.

Laing, O. (2020). *Funny Weather: Art in an Emergency*. London: Picador.

Phelan, P. (1999). *Unmarked: The Politics of Performance*. London: Routledge.

I

Precarity and vulnerability

1 Life on pause

Entanglements of the maternal and the mortal in a global pandemic

Katherine Nolan

Dr Katherine Nolan lectures in Creative Digital Media at Technological University Dublin. As an artist, she works primary in live and lens-based performance, exhibiting internationally in Europe, America, and Asia. She curates for *MART* and *Livestock Performance Art Platform.* Her practice-led research investigates gender and embodiment across live and digital contexts.

'Life on Pause' explores my experience as a mother and artist during the pandemic and its impact on my performance practice. The chapter examines *Fluid Flesh*, a visual art project through which I sought to unravel entangled affective embodied experiences of becoming a mother, whilst losing my own mother (to cancer). The project ascribes to feminist approaches that seek to account for and make visible lived experiences of motherhood through art practice (Mary Kelly, Mierle Laderman Ukeles, Lena Šimić, Aine Phllips, and Helena Walshe), as well as those that mobilise maternal embodiment as a way to rethink subjectivity and challenge the assumption of a Western singular, autonomous, rational, disembodied, and male universal subject (Bracha L. Ettinger, Hannah Arendt, Lisa Baraitser, Alison Stone, and Raphael-Leff). This analysis of practice took place at a point when the artwork was shifted into a new context. In the COVID moment, in which society has been suddenly, radically – if perhaps temporarily – reorientated, issues of care, interdependence, labour, and mortality became heightened concepts, bringing them into sharp focus. These are the very concerns of motherhood that I argue can be better understood through a maternal ontology.

O'Reilly and Green contend that 'mothering is the frontline of this pandemic' (2021, Cover copy). Paid and unpaid familial and community care is largely still considered women's work, meaning that the increased material and emotional pressure of societal shutdowns has borne down heavily on women and increased the invisible 'crisis of

DOI: 10.4324/9781003165644-3

motherwork' (O'Reilly and Green, 2021, Cover copy). In addition, many forms of oppression that may intersect with the experience of motherhood, such as those based on gender, race, ethnicity, disability, class, and age, have become amplified or even deadly, through the pandemic. Women have been disproportionally affected, their social roles and careers regressing globally as they 'manage the competing demands of care and wage labour' (Abstract Yildirim, Eslen-Ziya, 2020; Badri, 2020; Madgavkar et al., 2020; O'Reilly and Green, 2021, Cover copy; The Mothership Project, and Kara, 2021;).

Experiences of the maternal, mortality, and the pandemic are not unified or equal. Indeed, motherhood and the maternal are themselves problematic terms, which can essentialise, naturalise, and exclude (Underwood-Lee and Šimić, 2016: 6). In this chapter, I employ the specificity of my lived experience as a mother, academic, and performance artist, in order to interrogate intersecting issues of care, labour, and cultural work. This is one view of the maternal from a particular position: that of a white, Irish, middle-class, cis-gendered woman, living, and working in Dublin. Maternal experiences are rendered invisible, both as they are immaterial, undervalued, hidden, discounted, and disavowed; and because they are fluid, moving, and difficult to know or grasp. This chapter, eked out in the gaps that I could make between and through mothering, now becomes the mode by which my maternal experiences are rendered readable. In this way, the essay aims to reflect on the experience of a mother-maker impacted by the pandemic, as well as the reshaping of a performance practice through this rapidly changing context.

Fluid flesh: materiality, maternity, and mortality

Fluid Flesh seeks to unpack my experience of being pregnant for the first time, whilst my mother was terminally ill. The project began as a live performance, my first since my son was born, and was a gut reaction to the turmoil of these events. I envisioned an amorphous mass of flesh; an ambiguous bodily growth holding both potential and aberration. I materialised this with slime, a children's toy made especially popular via viral video. It is a semi-solid material, with a viscous plasticity and haptic visual appeal that I activate with my body in the artwork. The performance took place in the Contemporary Irish Arts Centre Los Angeles, a large warehouse space in Bergamot Station art complex in June 2019. In a burgundy-red mid-length dress, I lie on the polished concrete floor. As the audience enters, a glut of fleshy, pink, thick fluid with blue-veined streaks seeps across my waist and torso. It is cold and heavy. It bears down on me, pressing me to the floor, then flowing into my armpits and slowly spreading outwards. I am still. I am both laid out as a corpse in cold contact with ground, and laid on my back as if birthing, leaking, or excreting liquefied flesh.

My fingers begin to move, extricating themselves from the clingy, sticky fluid. Slowly, I rise and grasp a fistful of flesh. I pull forward and feeling the dragging weight of the substance as I rise. I gather the material in my arms, attempting to carry it across the gallery. It eludes my hold and pours down my body, streaming between my legs, leaving en/trails behind me on the floor. It is a touchable material and seems familiar to the children audience members, to the degree that they playfully gather it up and return it to me. A woman approaches me and moulds my body with slime breasts and belly, which then fluidly sag and fold as if ageing and decaying. I continue scooping and carrying the slime eventually culminating by angrily shaping a fleshy organ, beating it from hand to hand and thrusting it on the ground. I feel heavy with the body of slime now attached to my dress, the weight of which drags me downwards. I cut myself out of the mass and leave the aftermath on the floor. Over time, it dries and shrivels, twisting in form as it gnarls, like sunken skin receding from the bone.

Fluid Flesh seeks to reconcile the seemingly opposite and yet interrelated experiences of becoming a mother and losing a mother. They have become entangled as an affective node of experience buried in my flesh that I seek to unravel through performance. Handling the material, I provoke again the ambivalence of the comingled experiences of birth and death. The slime represents the rolling flesh of my body, my baby's body, and my mother's body. To be pregnant is to physically transform, but it is also to live with the potential of life and death at the same time. As I try to pull this semi-liquid in order to hold it against me, I move between holding a life, and grasping at a life it slips away from me. As I tussle with this substance, it comes to represent flesh at the threshold of 'aliveness'.

Thus, the slime represents the matter of the body in process, liquefying into fluid forces of change that hold both potential and terror. Sellberg and Aghtan assert that such bodily fluidity is a corporeality that is challenging to dominant western understandings of the body as stable and coherent, as well as normatively white, male, and non-disabled (2014). They argue that the concept of the body as solid obfuscates the fluid, mucousy, semi-permeable flows and exchanges of the body, through which rises a threatening, ungraspable, uncontainable corporeality (Sellberg and Aghtan, 2014: 166). My experiences of gestating a foetus and witnessing the death process are, equally, highly liquid moments; after all, bodily fluids circulate and pool atypically in pregnancy and death, and bodies coming into being, or going out of being, are moments of radical ontological instability. Thus, this semi-liquid, as a fluid, viscous, flesh became a way of grappling with the uncontainability of the body. *Fluid Flesh* was a material reliving of the ungraspable instability of both my pregnant body and my mother's dying body.

The performance with primordial slime also captures and provokes my lived experiences of mothering, of being umbilically tied and physically and emotionally entangled with another. The work mobilises the maternal body as both sensually bound and messily attached. As I try to hold the emergent matter, it rolls down my body, pools under my feet, and drags behind me in trails upon the floor. The dripping threads of flesh between my legs mark both the physical growths of pregnancy and birth and its aftermath; they are the pulling weight of attachment and maternal responsibility. The performance materialises acts of 'carriance' borne by the maternal body (Ettinger, 2015). That is, acts of carrying, inside and outside the body, through which Bracha L. Ettinger asserts (trans)subjectivity emerges. She argues that because bodies come into being within another body, the singularity of Western concepts of subjectivity dissolve against this maternal being wit(h)nessing (Ettinger, 2006). Through the lens of the maternal all subjectivity is rather trans-subjective and affectively produced through encounters with the m/Other (Ettinger, 2006: 41).

The act of carrying this flesh mobilises the carriance of trans-subjectivity as physical, burdensome and tangled. Karen Barad's concept of entanglements describes the messy, knotted nature of inter-relationality in which the distinguishable boundaries of subjects dissolve through their inter-actioning agencies (Barad, 2003). As a physical experience of affective bodily entanglement, the performance re-presents for me the binding bond that now characterises my existence, that is, my maternal ontology. It re-performs the lived experience of being physically and hormonally bonded and bound to my baby through pregnancy, birth, and nursing. It evokes the flow of milk and oxytocin, the weight I continually bear night and day, and the joy and jumble crawling about me and under my feet. It captures the messiness of my life and my thoughts and the extreme focus that the weight of responsibility brings. This life, this way of being, flowed before me and through me. It is sticky and thick and clings to my ribs, my insides, and my outsides. It is my baby and my body, and my mother and her mother.

Alison Stone describes the circularity of 'maternal time' (2012: 25). She draws on psychoanalyst Raphael-Leff's assertion that the exposure to the raw affects of the neonate and to maternal/neonatal bodily fluids viscerally returns the mother to her own pre-symbolic primal scene with her archaic mother (2009: 9). Stone asserts that the mother's psychic projecting of herself both backwards to her own past, and forwards to the present/future of her child, relationally structures maternal subjectivity. Thus,

> The mother is a relational subject, but doubly so: she inhabits two sets of relations transposed upon one another... To repeat the past with a difference is to cycle back through the past anew, and thus to experience under a cyclical form of temporality.
>
> (Stone, 2012: 25)

I find myself in this circularity of maternal time. I catch myself constantly bestowing acts and affects that my mother bestowed upon me. When I gently touch my baby's face, it is her touching mine. When I hear my child laugh and gawk at a mishap, I hear her laugh, that has passed through me to him. I hear my child laugh like my mother and uncannily feel I am both her and not her, that she is here and she is not here. Again, I find myself at the threshold of aliveness. This cyclicality, cycling back on the self as an existence within a physic past-present, is also part of grief. It is the way the shock of trauma constantly replays a past that is lost. My experience of gestation, birth, and neonatal care was transposed with my experience of grief. And thus my handling of this viscous material is too a cycling, an endless replaying of the fluidity and mortality of maternal flesh.

Care and labour in the COVID moment

This cyclicality continues as a new societal collective grief dawns through COVID-19 and new meanings become enfolded in the forms of the project. As I began to pull myself back to post-partum practice, the *Fluid Flesh* project is paused when the effect of the COVID-19 pandemic reached Europe. Irish society went into shutdown on 12 March 2020. Life was simultaneously on pause and fast-forward at the same time. My support systems, social interactions, daily habits, routines, and coping mechanisms abruptly fell away. With no childcare, I struggled to balance the care of my three-year-old, online teaching, and broader academic responsibilities. Amidst the frantic adjustment to the sudden shock of the pandemic, anything that was considered extraneous to subsistence fell away.

Stripped back to a nervous system of essential work, the societal crisis of the COVID moment was revealing. Forced to designate certain kinds of labour as essential to survival, the interdependence and yet inequality of societies was laid bare on local and global scales. Care and labour became heightened concepts. Formal and informal systems of care, invisible and undervalued came under pressure (medicine, nursing, social work, disability and mental health services, elder care, childcare, and community care). The disruption of the crisis revealed how much economies do not recognise their dependence on care work. It highlighted the need for society to entirely reconsider the value of care – value both in the sense of labour and in the sense of cherished societal principles. Jagoe and Kivland examine care as both an institutional and individual concept in the UK context. They assert how it has been co-opted by neoliberalist agendas as commodity, transaction, and political rhetoric, whist the care system simultaneously suffered the violence of recent austerity policies (2020). They argue that care needs to be radically reimagined and informed by an understanding of our inter-relationality. The shock of the pandemic crisis was a collective moment in which our interdependence was strongly felt, and yet blatant inequalities of gender, class, race, ethnicity, disability, and age were intensified. We must keep hold of this brief vision of our matrixial interdependence, to retain this cognisance of the weight borne by those who care, and of neglected social, economic, and affective needs.

The closure of many networks of care meant work-cum-childcare arrangements for many parents at home disproportionally fell on women. Childcare is largely rendered both non-work and women's work. Kathi Weeks asserts how 'the family and its ideology help to obscure the cost of productive labour by privatizing, feminizing, and naturalizing much of the work involved in its reproduction' (Weeks, 2011: 143). Cultural labour too is undervalued in capitalist societies ideological produced as pleasure rather than labour. It is underpaid or not paid and often has to be worked around other paid roles (Terranova, 2000: 36–37). Thus, in different ways, both maternal and cultural labour are not valued or are considered less valuable. They are rendered invisible while also being exploited for the profit that can be extracted. Experiences of contemporary westernised motherhood are often unpinned by a lived contradiction in which women are caught '*between the seductive/repellent pull/push of the baby's unmet needs*' and expectations of being an autonomous Western subject with its 'illusory separateness' (Raphael-Leff, 2009: 3 – original emphasis). Thus, mother who are makers – already pulled between the autonomy of work and the responsibility of childcare – bear a double burden, additionally contending with the material and psychological effects of their practices being considered of little value. The pressured, undervalued, unsupported, unrecognised aspects of mother-makers' lives, who were already playing multiple roles, squeezed into too little time, headspace, and energy, were further intensified through the pandemic.

The maternal and the mortal through the COVID-19 frame

When space eventually opened up to make art work, the *Fluid Flesh* project became reframed through these material circumstances and the pressure of physical and psychological containment. Plans to perform live for an exhibition in The Golden Thread Gallery in Belfast were stalled as it was no longer permissible to cross county borders. Instead, reperforming the work for camera became the focus of my practice. The ontology of the material had successfully captured the physical and psychological entanglement of motherhood, but it refused to be easily captured through the lens. I set about trying to discover how to record the qualities of this as ever-moving, indefinite and just plain sticky matter. I work the materials with my hands and notice its ability to take shape. A series of ambiguous bodily forms emerge as fleshly mounds and strings, organs and entrails. As I gently cup the flesh with both hands, it takes on a mirroring quality, becoming the left- and right-side of the brain, heart or lungs. Yet the malleability of this material is time-based. While it retains the memory of the body's touch, just as quickly the forms imprinted recede and these corporeal impressions melt away. I work to portray these temporal forms on camera, and they become a series of moving image works that animate the flesh as pulsing organs or organisms.

The material cathartically performs for me the body's relationship to time. Over time the body, which seems so existent, sensate and experiential, will seep out of form and into the nothingness of a primordial soup of cells. In order to make these forms come to life, I have to work against time to capture them before they dissolve. I animate them through the back and forward motion of the video such that they beat into life. Philip Auslander has argued that media simulates the liveness of performance through mimesis (1999). In the context of my work, media performs a mimetic aliveness by arresting the fleshy forms before they seep back into a pool of liquid. They are continually animated and yet never moving beyond their ability to replay the same moment. It is as if they have absorbed the conditions of life under COVID-19 and the limited momentum of subjects desperately seeking agency.

These audio-visual flesh works are a working through of lived embodied experiences as images and touchable objects. They are a remaking, reshaping, reconciling and resolving of forms and affects. They are the holding on to, and letting go of, life. The shaping of the flesh evokes both the forming of my son's heart within my body, supported by my circulatory system, and the holding of my mother's hand, as her heart fails and falls out of motion. The working of this material is a working through of the shock of birth, as well as that of grief. It materialises the vivid, embodied, affective knowledge that surfaces through witnessing the body in process as it forms out of, or returns into, amorphous cellular matter. The work summons the psychological space of grief and the incapacity to imagine mortality and the process of dying, through to trying to hold onto that which is ungraspable. Through this material process I ask, at what point do you cease to exist? At what point did I lose you, as I sat beside your bed and listened to your body changing? I clasped your hand, the circulatory system failing, as my body, and its rewired vascular system, circulated life blood to a growing, beating pulse.

As I write, I think of those experiencing or unable to experience their loved-one's life passing. Death and dying in COVID times has become a lonely activity, as we are starved of our ritual gathering together and the soothing care of being with one another, that is, the carriance through death and grief. Each individual death and the daily tolls constantly raise the spectre of our own mortality, both individual and collective. In the effort to keep ourselves alive through COVID-19, we must constantly imagine our deaths. The COVID moment, a context in which mortality is psychically, socially, and culturally ever-present, reframes this project and its summoning of maternal and mortal experience as moments of ungraspable corporeality. The mother's flesh – now transposed for the still and moving image – has morphed into organs and organisms, through which maternal embodied experience is connected to a global sense of the precarious morality of individuals, and of humans as a species.

As Irish society entered its third societal shutdown, life was once again paused, and along with it the *Fluid Flesh* project. These entangled experiences of the maternal and the mortal are made visible now only through this text. As with so much of life in this pandemic, through which we endure an ontology that is every changing shape.

This mode of existence demands mental and physical plasticity as we are pushed and pulled between the possibilities of life and its cessation. Under the pressure of the pandemic, societies are living through 'maternal time', a time that cycles back and forth, in which we are constantly returned to our interdependence, our mortality, and our ungraspable corporeality.

Artwork

Nolan, Katherine. *Fluid Flesh.* Live performance at *Contemporary Irish Arts Centre Los Angeles*, as part of *Care, Complicity, Critique*, 2019. Documentation available at www.katherinenolan.net/

References

Auslander, P. (1999). *Liveness: Performance in a Mediatized Culture.* London: Routledge.

Badri, B. (2020). The Impact of COVID-19 on Women. Available at: https://www.un.org/en/un-chronicle/impact-COVID-19-women [accessed 01/03/21].

Barad, K. (2003). Posthumanist Performativity: Toward an Understanding of How Matter Comes to Matter. *Signs: Journal of Women in Culture and Society*, 28(3), pp. 223–239. https://doi.org/10.1007/978-3-319-62140-1_19

Ettinger, B. L. (2006). *The Matrixial Borderspace.* Minneapolis: University of Minnesota Press.

Ettinger, B. L. (2015). Carriance, Copoiesis and the Subreal. In: S. Evren, ed., *SALTWATER: A Theory of Thought Forms.* Istanbul: 14th Istanbul Biennial, Istanbul Foundation for Culture and Arts, pp. 92–101.

Jagoe, R. and Kivland, S., eds. (2020). *On Care.* London: MA BIBLIOTHÈQUE.

Madgavkar, A., White, O., Krishnan, M., Mahajan, D., and Azcue, X. (2020). COVID-19 and Gender Inequality: Countering the Regressive Effects. Available at: https://www.mckinsey.com/featured-insights/future-of-work/COVID-19-and-gender-equality-countering-the-regressive-effects [accessed 01/03/21].

O'Reilly, A. and Green, F. J. (2021). *Mothers, Mothering, and COVID-19: Dispatches from the Pandemic.* Ontario: Demeter Press. https://doi.org/10.2307/j.ctv1h45mcj

Raphael-Leff, J. (2009). Maternal Subjectivity. *Studies in the Maternal*, 1(1), pp. 1–5. http://doi.org/10.16995/sim.159

Sellberg, K. and Aghtan, K. (2014). Being and Slime: An Alluvial Introduction. *InterAlia – A Journal of Queer Studies*, (9), pp. 166–185.

Stone, A. (2012). Maternal Memory and Lived Time. *Studies in the Maternal*, 4(1), pp. 1–26. https://doi.org/10.16995/sim.47

Terranova, T. (2000). Free Labor: Producing Culture for the Digital Economy. *Social Text*, 63, 18(2), pp. 33–58.

The Mothership Project, and Kara, H. (2021). The Mothership COVID Questionnaire. Available at: https://themothershipproject.wordpress.com/2021/01/31/our-mothership-project-COVID-survey/. [accessed 01/03/21].

Underwood-Lee, E. and Šimić, L. (2016). *Live Art and Motherhood: A Study Room Guide on Live Art and the Maternal.* London: Live Art Development Agency

Weeks, K. (2011). *The Problem with Work: Feminism, Marxism, Antiwork Politics, and Postwork Imaginaries.* Durham and London: Duke University Press.

Yildirim, T. M. and Eslen-Ziya, H. (2020). The differential impact of COVID-19 on the work conditions of women and men academics during the lockdown. *Gender Work Organisation*, 28(S1), pp. 243–249. https://doi.org/10.1111/gwao.12529

2 The impact of COVID-19 on freelance contemporary dance work

Precarity and the vulnerabilities of the dancing body

Lito Tsitsou

Dr Lito Tsitsou is a cultural sociologist interested in art, artistic production, ballet and contemporary dance, the moving body, film consumption, and Bourdieu's social theory. She is currently a Lecturer in Sociology at the University of Glasgow working on the impact of COVID-19 on dancers' work in Greece and the UK, 'specialised' film consumption across English regions with Professor Bridgette Wessels, and precarity in cultural industries and academia.

Since the beginning of the health crisis, the world of dance has been vocal about the challenges and consequences of the pandemic for institutions, choreographers, and performers alike, both through formal (see Bakare, 2020, Saha et al., 2020) and informal channels. Accordingly, I took an interest in documenting how freelance dancers and choreographers responded to the multiple crises generated by the pandemic. I was, specifically, concerned about their conditions of work, personal and artistic situations, their vulnerabilities, and anxieties. This chapter draws on six online interviews with freelance contemporary dance artists, based across the UK, discussing the impact of COVID-19 on their work. It explores their experiences of dealing with and working through the pandemic, their concerns, and responses.

Artists and dance scholars have begun to reflect on the differential impact of COVID-19 on dance communities by considering the shift in practices, performative means and styles of movement. Monteiro (2020) discusses efforts in adapting contemporary dance technique teaching during the first phase of lockdown at the University of Lisbon, exploring diverse approaches through Zoom. Weber (2020a and 2020b) identifies key challenges in dance digitalisation, namely the loss of contact and embodied practice, and the emerging identity and mental health crises. Furthermore, she discusses issues of equity in

DOI: 10.4324/9781003165644-4

dance education as influenced by this shift online. Heyang and Martin (2020) document key frustrations in adapting dancing and dance teaching to the digital sphere including its impact on dancers' physicality. Finally, Warnecke (2020) briefly, but systematically, maps the organisational and financial implications of the pandemic for stages and theatres, as well as the impact on cultural participation associated with the reduction and closure of venues. These primary texts pave the way for a deeper exploration of the consequences of the pandemic on embodied arts, and upon dance especially.

Similarly, I embarked on documenting such consequences by interviewing via Zoom six dance artists of various nationalities at different career stages: Nicky and Shona, both early career dancers and creatives; Penny, a mid-career dancer and choreographer; Beth and Jon, mid-career dancers and teachers; and Ruth, an established choreographer and teacher.[1] They practice different techniques, including contemporary ballet, Graham, release, contact improvisation, aerial dance, and fusion. All but one (Nicky) worked as dance teachers alongside their freelance work and have all remained relatively active during the various lockdowns.

A precarious dance: unstable working conditions and making ends meet during COVID-19

Dance artists' chief concerns were the volatile working conditions and the associated financial insecurity incited by the pandemic, as well as the coping strategies they developed in response. In March 2020, the national lockdown put an abrupt halt to creative activities and onstage performances, signalling the end of work for artists across the UK. Repercussions were immediately felt, as loss of income and decline in opportunities cemented a period of professional and financial instability for dancers and choreographers.

Even though freelance cultural labour has been historically unstable, intermittent, and financially insecure (Menger, 2006: 4), financial and existential precarity within the neoliberal conditions of artistic production is particularly acute (Cohen, 2013: 38; Ross, 2009: 4). The pandemic forged a further sense of precariousness for independent performers and choreographers with an abrupt shock-to-the-system decline of work and income. Artists in my sample experienced this differently depending on their personal circumstances and career stage, yet they reported considerable and often catastrophic reduction of earnings while they continue to experience financial uncertainty throughout the lockdown periods. Beth described her situation at the beginning of the pandemic as a total loss:

> When the pandemic hit, I had a whole year of work planned for one of the first times in a long time; when the pandemic hit everything stopped [...] I was left there with no work, very little money, and no prospect of earning.

Ruth another established artist, recounted:

> I relied quite heavily on 50% of my work being freelance, and all of it was lost overnight! So, there was a significant reduction in my earnings.

As these quotes testify, the intensity with which change was experienced, namely from work to no work and potentially no income, was overwhelming. Despite differences in their circumstances, all artists in this sample concurred that the impact has been detrimental. As Penny explained:

> I know people, now, working as couriers for Amazon in the dance world; and whether those people are able to come back to dance is a big question.

The possibility of stopping or changing jobs was one that all my interviewees had contemplated. Yet, this group has managed, so far, to eschew such prospects, thanks to mechanisms of support emerging throughout the lockdowns. Those with a longer trajectory in the field qualified for self-employment support or a hardship fund in England or Scotland. They also managed to retain some creative work and/or teaching (initially online), either as freelancers or in established institutions that employ them occasionally or on a part-time basis. Even though both were considered fundamental sources of financial assistance, for most artists these sources alone were insufficient. Thus, some found themselves in debt at least part of the time during the pandemic.

Freelance dance artists experience perpetual uncertainty about their own future financially as well as professionally. Shona, an early-career artist, stated that the future of dance is unclear, and therefore, an unstable industry to work in: ‘the future feels uncertain, and it doesn’t feel like a great industry to be in during these uncertain times’. Moreover, participants teaching at graduate level during the pandemic expressed concerns about the prospects of the upcoming generations of dancers and their chances of working professionally as performers, creatives, or educators in the future. Jon reflected:

> What kind of world they are coming into? Like the MBA programs I'm teaching now, what am I training them for? [...] that's a really big concern; and, financially, what job are they going to do?

Beth confirmed that these anxieties were already developing in professional schools:

> Students were struggling because they were graduating into a world where their profession – their potential profession – has died; so, they were working hard for potentially nothing and I had to be aware that they were feeling that way.

Indeed, this appears to have been the case for recent dance graduates in Nicky's circle, who stopped dancing in view of the lack of prospects and opportunities in the COVID-19 era.

However, for early-career performers, Nicky and Shona, dancing freelance already represented precarious, unstable work. Insecure, project-based work (Gill, 2002; Kong, 2011), scarce performances, low paid or unpaid work (Ursell, 2000), and increased competition for both residencies and places in small-scale productions are common at early career stages. These conditions apply across the performing arts, namely music and theatre, and legitimise a culture of low or no pay work for young artists (see Bain and McLean 2012; Lingo and Tepper, 2013; Umney and Kretsos, 2015). In that sense, young dancers' expectations of having an income are rather low; still, the pandemic enforced further scarcity of opportunities key to their development. As Shona explained:

> Straight away and before any lockdown was announced, work was already disappearing and very quickly projects were cancelled [...] I thought I would have a residency in December but that got put off...

This was also confirmed by Penny, a mid-career artist: 'I lost a residency this January, it was postponed for another time'.

Residencies offer freelancers, and especially early-career artists, the space to develop their own work and prepare for performance. These have become less available during the pandemic primarily due to space closures; hence the few remaining opportunities have become increasingly competitive. As Shona argued, 'applications have gotten far more competitive [...] we had 250 applications for five positions'.

Overall, this demonstrates a sharp decline in creative prospects in an already limited field of possibilities for younger performers. This forced both early-career dancers in my sample to move back with their parents in their respective home countries; a choice which has reportedly been made by most young artists in my participants' circles. Nicky and Shona managed to stay active during this time and pursued further study and teaching. Parental support was central to their capacity to remain engaged, with key provisions being space for training and teaching and financial help, whether direct or indirect. This shows that young and early-career dancers require assistance to remain operational (see Bynner, 2005 about familial support and youth in transition). Further, they are in a state of extended parental semi-dependency (Heath et al., 2008), what Stone et al. (2014) call 'boomerangs', especially during periods of crisis with reduced opportunities for work.

Nevertheless, participants emphasised the importance of professional networks as forms of provision during this period. As Oakley (2009: 31) argues, networks serve as means through which cultural workers manage the risks and uncertainties of work, and the associated emotional and psychological consequences of precariousness. In this sample, more established artists offered or received work or financial support from and to other dancers during the pandemic, which also benefited early-career artists.

Even though dancers and choreographers sustained some aspects of work and remained professionally and financially secure, the conditions under which this was endured were challenging. Scotland and England employed differential approaches to physical, face-to-face work at different points since the beginning of the pandemic, which for freelancers complicated things further. Those who worked in England (Nicky, Penny, Jon, and Beth) had more face-to-face opportunities, while work in Scotland was overall more restricted. Changes in regulations meant indefinite postponement or cancellation of performances and residencies often at very short notice, while artists were unable to respond to the frequent and abrupt shifts required within a restricted time frame. As Shona explained:

> The constant postponing, changing, adapting of projects makes your head spin; things change all the time and you're trying to keep up.

As a result, beyond the professional and financial precarity, the constant shifting of the landscape of cultural work intensified artists' sense of instability and risk.

Creative anxieties: how to produce dance in the pandemic?

Linked to the shifting conditions of access to work and income, dance artists reported great anxiety, both individually and collectively, about the format of creative work, as well the type of artistic outputs produced. The limitations posed by the lockdown and the lack of 'live work' are seen to engender questions for the future of dance making and performance. Specifically, concerns were raised regarding the type of work produced because of venue closures, such as screen dance or film, often included in some of the present performers and makers' portfolios. Digital and film dance may be an interesting direction, but not necessarily one that all artists would like to pursue. As Shona observed, 'not everyone got on the digital bandwagon'.

The limitations of digital work are felt, as the artistic and creative possibilities of physical work are declining. Jon queried whether film could undermine live work in the future, and what this could entail for physical engagement. Specifically, he posed the question:

> Why, why does it always have to be a film now? And of course, it does, but I wonder what that says about the nature of live movement?

Equally, younger dancers appeared particularly worried about access to traditional contemporary dance performance and wondered how physical work could be reinstated post COVID-19.

This has serious implications for dancing and choreographing. As Weber (2020a: 4) states, 'Dance is an inherently embodied art form – even when abstracted, our sense of movement comes from an embodied awareness'. Specifically, touch and close contact is a key means of traditional dance-making and performance, which has been severely curtailed during the pandemic. All artists highlighted the importance of and creative need for bodily connections in contemporary dance. Jon and Ruth reflected on the centrality of physical contact and touch in choreographing and performing as affective and creative dimensions of dance. Ruth explained:

> It's a huge thing in our experience as dancers, it is a very healing thing and it's part of that community bonding [...] I've had many dance partners with whom I've pas de deuxed and we touched, [...]

> and it's a connection that makes you really feel, over time, that you don't know where one person stops and the other person begins.

When bodies become the dance, there is a constant creative and performative flow emanating from, and directed towards, dancing bodies, whether in pairs or en masse. This form of connectedness is linked both to the aesthetic, communicative, and technical aspects of dancing (Fraleigh, 1987). In other words, it is fundamental to performance as a practice, but also as a spectacle. What is more, it constitutes an affective state as well as a skill. As Jon argued:

> As a dancer working in duets in contact improvisation, that sensitivity, how to read and how to feel another body in terms of flesh, bone – that is such an important part of honing that skill, so I worry about that.

Nicky and Beth – the only artists involved in face-to-face rehearsals during a gap between lockdowns – described the enjoyment of dancing and working next to other bodies especially after some time away from performance. As Nicky stated, 'We were all happy and passionate and we all enjoyed it'.

Creative anxieties: space, movement, and physical creativity

The abrupt stoppage of staged performance stalled artists' work in progress and limited choreographers' capacity to experiment with movement in space and construct dance. Equally, dancers were left with no room to rehearse or perform. What this revealed, beyond the inevitable decline of creative work, was the interconnectedness of space and movement for creative purposes, which has been entirely or excessively curtailed during the pandemic. Artists moved into confined spaces (Weber, 2020a), usually their homes, where they attempted to practice. Out of the six artists I spoke to, only half had sufficient room inside their home, while the need for safe and suitable spaces such as studios and rehearsal rooms increased.

This shift, from specialised spaces to domestic ones, exposed dancers' bodies as creative instruments into various challenges. Jon expressed his frustration over working in a confined space:

> This is my studio, my little kitchen; it's got a stone floor and I can touch the ceiling with my hands [...] I'm really getting sick of ricocheting around these four walls; I feel like a pinball. I can't use my

> full extension; I can't use my full shift [...] I really miss traveling in one direction.

Penny also stated:

> I realised I hadn't been jumping. It's hard to jump, if you live in a flat when you are concerned about your neighbour downstairs, you can't do lots of it [...] and of course there is the safety issue; I couldn't dive into the floor, I can't do that in my lounge.

These quotes highlight the limitations posed on the dancing body as it becomes spatially challenged and physically constrained. Penny explained further:

> You can rehearse at home – like you can remember the material, but if it's meant to be done in space that's four-five times the size of your lounge and you'll need to jump, it's just not possible!

This sense of physical but also creative restriction was further intensified by the shift to online work. Beth expressed her frustration about attempting to dance and create at home, which resulted in refusing to engage with online work beyond the necessary classes for physical preservation.

Overall, the impact of confinement had serious consequences on the creative possibilities for both dancers and choreographers across the sample.

Physical anxieties and bodily vulnerabilities

These concerns about the style and extent of movement also mirror performers' anxieties about their physical wellbeing. Dancing is linked to physical performance at optimum level. All artists (dancers and choreographers alike) spend a considerable part of their day rehearsing, taking or giving classes, and developing work. This daily routine was taken for granted before the pandemic. Yet COVID-19 entailed reduction of physical activity and bodily re-adjustment to scaled-down space inside homes, which had visible effects on practitioners' bodies. Nicky acknowledged:

> Physically, I haven't been at my best – there were phases where I was [during the pandemic] but, overall, I am not like I was before.

All artists observed their declining stamina and loss in the extent of movement they were able to perform before the pandemic. Worries about injury, recovery, and capacity to reclaim the breadth of movement lost were also expressed. Ruth elaborated:

> At first, I went through working out in my dance studio and stayed fit for about a term; then I noticed the decline in my fitness; […] everything just feels so different to what you're used to […] you take your first little triplet across the room and your hamstring aches, it kind of depresses you, because you've never been there as a dancer, that stuff was taken for granted.

Shona argued:

> When you're not at your strongest the injuries play up more, […] I've had a knee injury that's played up a lot more just because my legs aren't as strong as they were before.

Beth also noted that her body reacted to the decrease of movement with pains and old injuries resurfacing, while Nicky stressed that limited access to training in suitable space made dancers more prone to injury and their return to intensive work challenging.

Physical vulnerability and decline epitomise artists' ontological anxiety (see Duarte, 2020: 28–34). As bodily activity is central to the definition and practice of dance, concerns about the capacity to perform or the possibility of stopping threaten artistic identity. Artists expressed their worries about this in various ways, but by primarily acknowledging the possibility of stopping and the wider decline in the number of practitioners. Beth argued:

> I'm not leaving but I'm fully accepting that something might not happen; so, where does that leave me? and I'm kind of in that limbo, and I am fully accepting I am in that limbo […]

Penny explained, 'I definitely see people moving away from the art or into other areas', whilst Jon and Nicky agreed that 'there's going to be less of us in the future'. This was considered a serious consequence of the pandemic, and one that is already manifesting.

Anxieties about the body were also linked to online work. All but two interviewees (Nicky and Beth) have moved their work online, although both were involved in some form of digital work at least once.

This intense digitalisation of dance ranging from teaching, to creating and performing, awakened new physical challenges for practitioners. As Ruth explained:

> Choreographing much of the time digitally and over Zoom, we're really having to think about the fact it's very difficult to learn in this medium [...] but I also choreographed shows that were meant to be in person and were taken online and suddenly you know you're working with a theatre and a creative team and a performer in their bedroom, and it becomes very frustrating after a while.

As bodies become digital representations on screen, they lose their materiality and, with it, the physical connection between them; kinaesthetic empathy as well as the capacity to physically understand how muscular systems move diminishes. This concerns particularly the connection between dance partners, as discussed earlier, but also between teachers/choreographers and performers. Recreating movement safely from afar becomes particularly challenging. Beth lends her experience of working on a solo tailored on her body choreographically and the difficulties she experienced as a result:

> They made a solo on me over Zoom in my house and got so frustrated with the fact that I couldn't break through the wall. They were like 'I need to see this in space [...] I need to see you move' [...] Within the first five minutes, they asked me to do a full hinge to the floor and I was like cool! I have been *sitting on a sofa for weeks!*

This exemplifies choreographers and performers' lack of experience in creating via digital means and for digital purposes while engaging the body. However, dancers and choreographers alike accepted that digital work would continue for the foreseeable future, while onstage performance will be less available.

Conclusion

The pandemic has had complex consequences for freelance contemporary dance artists, revealing their precarious position as professionals, creatives, and dancers. The COVID-19 health crisis destabilised further their conditions of work and income and complicated creative possibilities through confinement and reduction of physical engagement. Even though online work became the primary form of dance production during the various periods of lockdown since March 2020, this had serious consequences for the physical and creative aspects of performance, generating questions about the future of dance as well as the future of its practitioners.

Note

1 Participants are referred to by pseudonyms with their consent to protect their anonymity. Two have agreed for their first name to be used, but I will not clarify who, to further ensure they are not identifiable. Care has been taken throughout the paper to make sure that participants' identities remain protected. This research was reviewed by the Ethics Committee of the College of Social Sciences, University of Glasgow (A/N 4002000097).

References

Bain, A. and McLean, H. (2012). The Artistic Precariat. *Cambridge Journal of Regions, Economy and Society*, 6(1), pp. 93–111. https://doi.org/10.1093/cjres/rss020.

Bakare, A. (2020). An Industry in Freefall: UK Dance Sector Calls for Urgent Help. *The Guardian*. 5 May. Available at: https://www.theguardian.com/stage/2020/may/05/coronavirus-threat-to-future-of-dance-lauren-cuthbertson-royal-ballet/ [accessed 01/03/2021].

Bynner, J. (2005). Rethinking the Youth Phase of the Life-course: The Case for Emerging Adulthood? *Journal of Youth Studies*, 8, pp. 367–384.

Cohen, N. S. (2015). Cultural Work as a Site of Struggle: Freelancers and Exploitation. In: C. Fuchs and V. Mosco, eds., *Marx and the Political Economy of the Media*. Leiden: Brill. pp. 36–64. DOI: 10.1163/9789004291416_004

Duarte, M. A. (2020). Artists' Precarity in the Context of Their Social Integration. In: T. Rachwał, R. D. Hepp and D. Kergel, eds., *Precarious Places Social, Cultural and Economic Aspects of Uncertainty and Anxiety in Everyday Life*. Wiesbaden: Springer VS. pp. 19–39.

Fraleigh, S. H. (1987). *Dance and the Lived Body: A Descriptive Aesthetics*. Pittsburgh: University of Pittsburgh Press.

Gill, R. (2002). Cool, Creative and Egalitarian? Exploring Gender in Project-based New Media Work in Euro. *Information, Communication & Society*, 5, pp. 70–89.

Heath, A., Rothon, C., and Kilpi, E. (2008). The Second Generation in Western Europe: Education, Unemployment, and Occupational Attainment. *Annual Review of Sociology*, 34, pp. 211–235.

Heyang, T. and Martin, R. (2020). A Reimagined World: International Tertiary Dance Education in Light of COVID-19. *Research in Dance Education*, DOI: 10.1080/14647893.2020.1780206

Kong, L. (2011). From Precarious Labor to Precarious Economy? Planning for Precarity in Singapore's Creative Economy. *City, Culture and Society*, 2(2), pp. 55–64.

Lingo, E. and Tepper, S. J. (2013). Looking Back, Looking Forward: Arts-Based Careers and Creative Work. *Work and Occupations*, 40(4), pp. 337–363. https://doi.org/10.1177/0730888413505229

Menger, P. M. (2006). Artistic Labor Markets: Contingent Work, Excess Supply and Occupational Risk Management. In: V. A. Ginsburgh and D. Throsby, eds., *Handbook of the Economics of Art and Culture Vol. 1.* Amsterdam: North-Holland/Elsevier Science. pp. 765–811.

Monteiro, E. (2020). How to Deal with Dance Technique When Home is our Stage. In: A. Moura, C. Almeida and M. H. Vieira, eds., *Diálogos com a Arte - Revista de Arte, Cultura e Educação*, 8 (December), pp. 86–94.

Oakley, K. (2009). *'Art Works' – Cultural Labour Markets: A Literature Review.* London: Creativity, Culture and Education.

Ross, A. (2009). *Nice Work If You Can Get It: Life and Labor in Precarious Times.* New York: New York University Press.

Saha, K., et al. (2020). An Open Letter to the Culture Secretary from Black, Asian & Ethnically Diverse Theatre Artistic Directors and Cultural Leaders on the Importance of Protecting Representation in the Sector. Available at: https://www.youngvic.org/blog/open-letter-from-black-asian-ethnically-diverse-theatre-artistic-directors?fbclid=IwAR1ZWYvmbyGhBLizKvP-KIZo6PDY77RcnRt1-WoFbfVrwdJbGsC_PPxcsUks [accessed 01/03/2021].

Stone, J., Berrington, A., and Falkingham, J. (2014). Gender, Turning Points, and Boomerangs: Returning Home in Young Adulthood in Great Britain. *Demography*, 51, pp. 1–20.

Umney, C. and Kretsos, L. (2015). 'That's the Experience': Passion, Work Precarity, and Life Transitions among London Jazz Musicians. *Work and Occupations*, 42(3), pp. 313–334.

Ursell, G. (2000). Television Production: Issues of Exploitation, Commodification, and Subjectivity in UK Television Labour Markets. *Media, Culture and Society*, 22, pp. 805–825.

Warneke, L. (2020) Art and Performance During the Time of COVID-19 Lockdown. *Agenda*, 34(3), pp. 145–147, DOI: 10.1080/10130950.2020.1783889

Weber, R. (2020a). Moving Embodied Practices Online: Editorial. Activist History Review. Available at: https://activisthistory.com/2020/10/02/moving-embodied-dance-practices-online/

Weber, R. (2020b). Social (Distance) Dancing during Covid with Project Trans(m)it. Available at: (https://researchspace.auckland.ac.nz/bitstream/handle/2292/53340/Weber%20Social%20Distance%20Dancing%20-%20TDPT%202020.pdf?sequence=3&TSPD_101_R0=2b8befe7a6c184eadae13298122e774fk71000000000000000058e1402effff00000000000000000000000000603cd83d00419014510850ab25feab2000c53d3fedc3961ae984188e52810c21cddc5bf3aa15c541ebae37f08c6f93a9c2086a9cec8e0a280036b30da94346bd31c4dca6a07f9b58a692b52823592f9064053a72201a96b3fdece9307db85b0c95) [accessed 01/02/2021].

3 Embrace your vulnerability

Cultivating art, theatricality, and performativity in times of catastrophe

Denise Espírito Santo and David Gutiérrez Castañeda

Denise Espírito Santo is Associate Professor of Art Education at the Arts Institute of UERJ; Professor at the Postgraduate Program in Arts and Contemporary Culture – PPGARTES; she holds a PhD in Literary Theory from UFRJ (2002), a Master's in Brazilian Literature from UFRJ (1994), and a Bachelor's Degree in Theater Theory from Uni-Rio (1996).

David Gutiérrez Castañeda is a sociologist at the National University of Colombia (2006), has Master's and Doctorate in History of Art from National Autonomous University of México (2011), is full-time Associate Professor in Art History at the National School of Higher Studies (ENES), UNAM, and is the winner of the National Prize of Art Criticism of the Colombian Ministry of Culture 2010 and author of the book *Mapa Teatro 1987–1992* (2014).

In the history of the invasions of the Americas, the figure of the mercenary-gunman-*capanga* has always played a crucial role, whether looting, committing violence against indigenous peoples, or destroying ecosystems. He is embedded within the politics of segregation, sexism, and racism. He is associated with the abusive exercise of power by the owners of the land – the minions of capitalism. This figure continues to play an important role in postcolonial contexts: he endures, even when the old plantation scenario gives way to other landscapes. Today, he appears in the capitalist environment of contemporary societies, where insurers, mineral and agricultural extractivist economies, banks, and stock exchanges function as privileged spaces for the emergence of the new gunmen and intrepid foremen-boys of the international financial system. Only the packaging has changed. Once portrayed as the tough guy, a typical paternal figure, 'lord of the plantation' in his white linen suit and Panama hat, the new representative of the feudal domain is clad in a starched shirt and tie. He charges

DOI: 10.4324/9781003165644-5

robust commissions for dirty work done with the usury of the State, sometimes showing off false qualifications, or degrees obtained from the best international universities. However, what remains is the abusive and colonial power he exerts, that has bled our territories dry for at least 500 years.

Now comes the COVID-19 pandemic, which has momentarily jammed the gears of the system. Late-stage capitalism is able to anticipate the extermination of humanity, contributing with its predatory logic to a rampant state of sterility and the exhaustion of energy and animistic resources, of the very soul of the world. The resulting public health crisis demonstrates that, once again, in the history of the great pandemics, our bodies are presented as the enclave of disease. We are simultaneously the sender and receiver of a virus that, if not universally lethal, is capable of spreading at dizzying speed to other bodies. As Cameroonian philosopher Achille Mbembe (Mbembe and Bercito 2020) put it, the pandemic democratised the power to kill.

However, COVID-19 is not the same as SARS-CoV-2, which is its agent. The virus is not 'the enemy'. Differentiating virus from disease is key; it allows us to distinguish cautious actions regarding how the virus behaves and is assembled from how colonial governance regimes administer and decide upon processes of healing. All of us have been sick at some point in our lives: indeed, healing is life itself. Yet, the minions of capitalism generate collateral slaughter to support the markets. The impossibility of stopping, taking time to create new criteria, the reality of structural economic precarity, the immunologies imposed by salary conditions, the rejections of indigenous knowledge, the impossibility to freely exercise one's rights, the historical negligence of states over the mechanisms and instruments of health, age, and racial, gender, and class privileges, all impact upon how, who, and under what conditions it is possible to heal. Assemblies demand attention in relation to the virus; likewise, colonial violence has guided how life is, how it should be lived, and who can be healed.

Indeed, the presence of the virus intensifies the violence of colonial powers. Infection is the relationship that our bodies establish with the virus, and this symbiosis is crucial when considering conditions of racial, gender, and economic justice. What COVID-19 reveals, according to Silvia Rivera Cusicanqui (2020), is the 'sneeze of Pachamama'. It is crucial, therefore, to understand that management of the pandemic can become a weapon that destroys human and more-than-human lives, a circumstance that somehow finds a parallel with the genocidal agenda of late-stage capitalism.

Some of us – approximately a third of the world's population – remain confined, even a year after the emergence of the virus. In Brazil and Mexico, respectively, we experience life as if in another time frame, which appears in opposition to the productivist rhythm that rules us – cities are now free from the noise of cars, planes, sirens, and the effects of soot and carbon monoxide. Despite this, high rates of urban waste, the permanence of oil-based energy consumption, increases in garbage dumping, the prohibitive prices of food, and technological infrastructure amidst the pandemic, all serve to exacerbate the violent discrepancy between rich and poor. For these contradictory reasons, these days have been, in a sense, better for Pachamama. However, where other worlds are coexisting with more-than-human species, life reaffirms itself and shows an impressive capacity for resilience in different ecosystems, perhaps reactivating complex protobiological chains that are most affected by the poisoning process against Mother Nature. But what scenarios lie in wait for the health crisis and resulting social isolation?

At the least expected moment, but at the most necessary and timely ever; from the most unexpected ontological place, the Earth has been politically convulsed and has yet to react. Like a subtle and paradoxical historical and geological earthquake, the coronavirus has changed everything, not with sudden movements, but with a massive and global paralysis. Its emergence in human biology has caused a major interpellation to the contemporary global population in its entirety, probably the most critical challenge that we have had to face in the short span of our adventure as a species (Aráoz, 2020).

COVID-19 aggravates the terminal state of an economic model and a global culture that is responsible for millions of infections and deaths worldwide. We can but hope that some of the resources to cope with mass unemployment brought about by COVID-19 will come from the imposition of great fortunes that continue accumulating. Indeed, perhaps some global platform will seek transparency and reallocate all the hidden and evaded money, as well as other practices to which the ruling classes systematically resort throughout the planet. At the top of the social pyramid sits a very small group of people – mainly white men. Their fortunes are growing exponentially, and today these billionaires have accumulated greater wealth than 4.6 billion people, that is, 60% of the world population – this is, surely, a glaring obscenity.

What post-pandemic scenarios might enable us to invent new ways of being-with, of putting into practice other protocols with the purpose of preventing a return to the previous state of affairs? What can and should be activated in this post-pandemic recovery, in the field of interpersonal relationships, in remote and telematic devices, in ecosystems? Why art in this context? How to invent new ways of doing theory and science? How to reinvent public space?

A tiny inhabitant of this planet, who lives only on the condition of being housed in other, more complex organisms, has managed to do what many, millions, would have wanted: a massive world strike that cut, for an indefinite time, the chains of exploitation; the exploitation of bodies and territories. That stopped the *maquilas* who plunder capacities; the chainsaws that destroy the forests; the fishing boats that sail the seas; harvesters that shear the soil; explosives that blow up mountains and squeeze rocks out of the ground (Aráoz, 2020).

Coming from this place of reverie and imagination, force fields will be activated by restoring lives. The only fragile certainty that we now have is that we cannot go back to what we were before. This is the case for many reasons, the first being the most challenging: we need to imagine once again, and give room for a full flourishing, even though our intuitions, affections and perceptions already understand their own presence. And it is from here that we want to assert the importance of generating other care repertoires.

Building on the ideas of Joan Tronto (1993) and María Puig de la Bellacasa (2017), we consider that care practices generate everything we do to maintain, continue, and repair the worlds we share. These worlds include everything we try to weave into a complex web that sustains life. This concept of 'worlds', plural, refers to a series of contingent situations, specific and entangled ecologies of human and more-than-human, animated and inanimate relationships. It is the intertwining (required or optional) and use of persistent entities and actions that keep us together, allow us to emancipate ourselves, and, in turn, enable the perpetuation and renewal of lives. Recognising the need for care goes beyond interhuman relationships; it is something that penetrates, challenges, causes discomfort, and forces us to do something. Caring is guiding efforts that intensify awareness, affection, and action bodily, assuming that, as beings and entities, we depend on each other.

To care is repetitive and reiterative. It works in support chains and requires a great deal of energy. It creates atmospheres and processes for the survival and reproduction of the liveable, not necessarily surplus value or products. But these practices can also be reclaimed by capitalism. Therefore, they are critical, relational, complex, historical, contingent, contradictory, and, above all, situated. Caring is doing, but it is also a debate.

Care practices have gained semantic density in this pandemic time, and this has led to redemptive narratives that have continued to insist on sexist, racist, discriminatory parameters, and invisible obligations. They addressed women, mothers of families, precarious and racialised people, health professionals, and others. The pandemic has been in charge of usurping care to support many hegemonies, beginning with those that are attractive to the servants of capitalism. However, it has also been a fertile territory to cultivate potentialised lives, generate experimental immunologies, dense affects, and survival actions. It has not been easy. Many of us are highly fragmented, economically and mentally impoverished. We are vulnerable to governments that analyse how many human and more-than-human lives are likely to perish to sustain their projects of profit and power. Even so, ingenuity, creation, communities, critical practices in multiple and intensive dimensions, in networks both at home and professionally have emerged.

By announcing some measures of protection for their villages and territories, violently threatened by the genocidal policies of Bolsonaro's government in Brazil, indigenous peoples have tried to concentrate efforts and publicise care actions, the objective of which is to denounce the project that tenant vultures: the genocide of indigenous peoples and the occupation of their territories with the purpose of a fiercer new stage of predatory exploitation. Actions consist of obstacles, complaints to the International Criminal Courts about the dismantling of public policies that represented some guarantee, and widespread use of social networks for the social mobilisation of this resistance and confrontation. One project in particular catches our attention: a video made by women of different ethnicities who also seek to emphasise ways of cultivating potential lives; 'embrace your vulnerability' thus gains strength through the voices of Yawalapiti, Kikatege, Pankararu, Terenas, Taurepang, Kaxuyana, Xakirabá, and Guajajaran women. Inspired by these stories, we propose to make a memory of these efforts, to mark the coordinates of their possibilities, and to spread them virulently.

References

Aráoz, H. M. (2020). Pandemia: sintomatología del Capitaloceno. *Lobo Suelto!* 22 April. Available at: http://lobosuelto.com/capitaloceno-virus-machadoaraoz/

Mbembe, A. and Bercito, D. (2020). Pandemia democratizou poder de matar, diz autor da teoria da "necropolítica". *Folha de S.Paolo*. 30 March. Available at: https://www1.folha.uol.com.br/mundo/2020/03/

pandemia-democratizou-poder-de-matar-diz-autor-da-teoria-da-necropolitica.shtml [accessed 09/07/2020].

Puig de la Bellacasa, M. (2017). *Matters of Care: Speculative Ethics in More Than Human Worlds*. Minneapolis: University of Minnesota Press.

Rivera Cusicanqui, S. (2020). Resistencias, insurgencias y luchas por la vida en tiempos de exterminios. *CLACSO TV*. 27 May. *YouTube*. Available at: https://www.youtube.com/watch?v=VQ08llpL9YM&t=18s&ab_channel=CLACSOTV/

Tronto, J. (1993). *Moral Boundaries: A Political Argument for an Ethic of Care*. London: Routledge.

4 *The Tenders*

Cover to cover – liner notes

Judd Morrissey and Mark Jeffery (ATOM-r) in collaboration with Abraham Avnisan

Judd Morrissey is a writer and code artist who creates poetic systems across a range of platforms incorporating electronic writing, internet art, live performance, and augmented reality. He teaches at the School of the Art Institute of Chicago and co-founded the performance collective Anatomical Theatres of Mixed Reality (ATOM-r).

Mark Jeffery is a performance/installation artist, curator, and Associate Professor at the School of the Art Institute of Chicago. Mark co-founded ATOM-r in 2012 a performance/technology group where he is a choreographer and performer in the company. He is a former member of Goat Island Performance Group.

Abraham Avnisan is an interdisciplinary artist whose work is situated at the intersection of image, text, and code. He has presented and performed his work both nationally and internationally. Abraham is an Assistant Professor of Emerging Media & Technology and Journalism & Mass Communication at Kent State University.

Side A

1 Rhinestone Cowboy (Dazzling Camouflage)
2 Beautiful Holy Jewel Home
3 The Discoverers (they wrote)
4 A Meat Empire has Wider Teeth
5 The Penumbra of Our Embrace

Side B

6 The Other Side of the Animal
7 Tender Embrasures Endanger Me
8 Each Breath Dilates the Window's Duration
9 Sailor's Handshake
10 Violence is the Tender's Embrace

DOI: 10.4324/9781003165644-6

11. Make you an Outfit (after Thomas Morrissey)*

* Bonus Track

*

A nudie suit is a way of covering while becoming uncovered

We set out to make a record with only a jacket so that the lines of each song could become part of its lining. Later there were two jackets, one gold and the other black, one thrusting its hips violently in the wind, and the other brushing its tassels on the ruins of the fort while refracting the light that pierces embrasures, creating both disco and nocturne.

We found ourselves heeding the call to unmake a record, to invert and penetrate the hollow shells of buildings not so much as substitute for hedonism but to open portals to the impossibility of an origin.

We stayed in to make a record that is the interiority of drapery furnishing the roominess of ligatures.

We knew that to cover a song was also to paper the bent plumb lines of a loneliness with rhinestone mosaics and a plumage fringe.

Yet we could not have anticipated that the *we* of bands and shared housing and orgies would become the networked *I*'s of persistent solitary fortification relieved by telepresence and telepathy.

The fort's disappearance became a fort by the same name

When I wandered the former Cold War military grounds and saw a boy leaning against a tree, giving himself to a group of bare-faced chasers, my desire was deterred by a distance measured in sleeve-lengths that dressed and addressed me.

The tree's encodings trace its history of the land from the birth of its roots but not before.

In the profile of my torso, its location was auto-detected as *Fort Dearborn Addition, Illinois.*

Original

getting cards and letters from people I don't even know

Cover

Where our missiles become missives from submissives we don't even know

We forgot that our windows are embrasures still

When this 'album' began we were looking at the meticulously rhinestoned home of Loy Bowlin, the *original rhinestone cowboy,* as a cover of Glen Campbell's 1975 hit.

Later, we were working in residence at the tender house of a mechanical bridge situated on the grounds of the former colonial Fort Dearborn.

The outer wall has a bas relief called *Defense,* commemorating the fallen fort, first destroyed in an indigenous uprising; then dismantled when its work was complete, still to haunt the land and nation in parcels of privatized space slyly retaining its name; and situated in proximity to a tower beaming with the gaudy ligatures of a rogue president.

The rectilinear parcels of the rogue fort are encircled by a tortuous looping of scratches and deep cuts comprising the story not told by the manufactured grooves of the bridge's cogs, as its peeling bell-sound rises to become one wall of a fortification to enclose the looting that is also a counter narrative to this museum's didactic:

The beaver's downfall was its excellent coat (Bridgehouse Museum, n.d.)

– Judd Morrissey

*

The pandemic Angels that can no longer close their wings --
This storm is what we call progress

Abe, Judd, and I wanted to make an uncanny world where strange augmented reality letters visualized as bricks from an 18th-century fort in Louisiana appear in one another's homes and backyards and then disappear into and onto our bodies as portals and voids that are danced on like glimmering beings. I want the world to dance on itself and embody itself. That the imagined is between worlds of real, surreal, and desire. To cry dance through a space of isolation and to open a doorway for the Rhinestone Cowboy to enter and hear the songs of two men singing through the network.

A head of waves, laughter dreams. Slipping into bowls of glimmer. Dancing in surreal desire, hands mark and touch. I want to glide on worlds imagined. And disappear within the murmurs. We were mining for ways to find a key that would unlock the virtual gateway and allow a stranger to come into our homes. Our homes have become homes and more: classrooms, offices, rehearsal spaces, gyms, stages, restaurants, dance halls, studios, forts, libraries, and sounds of a drawbridge being raised. Since March 13 of last year, I have been home, alone, with two cats – then, late summer, another cat arrived, Basil. I have left the neighborhood of this Ukrainian Village home perhaps four times in the last almost 11 months. I used to bike 60 miles a week. Movement stopped. Bed to coffee shop. To sit on a chair and hold space and activate permission and worlds through rectangular windows.

Abe, Judd, and I were searching for ways to communicate through this televirtuality to find a new language of movement that is layered and complex. How do you traverse one another's homes, upside down data, mapped Chicago inverted, fall into the guts of Trump Tower, wipe down the cracks of a bas relief that tells a story of settlers' progress that you do not wish to be repeated. We try to understand and listen. This task is difficult, the awkward silence on Zoom, the gaps.

Through our work we often posed the question: What is it to examine and reimage the landscapes/structures we have lost during the pandemic or in our own histories? I keep thinking about dance, televirtuality, to guide, to support, to assist in impossibility. The portal, the gap, the way the Lidar scans, the green screen materials of the house: Loy Bowlin's Dazzling Jewel home, fort, bridge, tower, and sites of the past. I think of Abe, Judd, and I entangled in the history of two French paintings.

We have become *The Gleaners*, the 1857 painting by Millet of working-class women picking the last bits of straw from the field after it had been harvested. We gathered; made a collection of unknown fragments; turned our field back into the home; and became floor scrapers, field, soil, floorboards, scratching, and scraping between worlds. We learnt to peel back the walls, to see forts and embrasures, to repair with glitter and tinsel augmented language as if placing Band-Aids and plasters onto the walls of our homes.

– Mark Jeffery

*

February 14, 2020. It is Valentine's Day & I am wearing tights in the backstage area of Fullerton Hall at the Art Institute of Chicago, attending to my inbreath/outbreath/inbreath, trying to calm my nerves in the long short minutes leading up to our stepping out from behind the curtain. We are about to perform *The Tenders* in front of a live audience of over 300 people.

We couldn't know then that a work we thought we were making about the past & present, about cowboys & rhinestones & cover songs & the American dream & the American nightmare & colonial forts & 20th century lift bridges & racist monumental sculptures & dispossessed indigenous nations & white supremacy as origin & telos was also a work about the year to come.

We couldn't know then that Valentine's Day 2020 would be our last in-person performance before the pandemic; before attending to our breath would become a matter of life & death; before George Floyd's breath was taken away forever; before the uprising for racial justice that followed demanding we never forget his heartbreaking last words *I can't breathe*; before Lori Lightfoot, mayor of Chicago, raised all the bridges in downtown Chicago to create a fortress protesters would be unable to escape from; before statues all over the world celebrating slave owners & colonizers would be toppled; before the epic, unprecedented assault on American Democracy that began with a lie & ended with violent insurrection at the US Capitol on January 6, 2021. 'A storm is blowing from Paradise… This storm is what we call progress,' Walter Benjamin writes of the Angel of History (Benjamin, 1969: 249).

White supremacy as origin & telos: that is the story of progress in the United States of America, & that will continue to be, unless we rise up & take control of our collective futures. As a cis, white, queer, Jewish, American/Israeli man—citizen & heir to not one but two settler-colonial societies—I know that I bear a special responsibility in this regard. As an artist, I strive to bear that responsibility in the best way I know how, by bringing it into the work. To borrow a line from Allen Ginsburg, one of my first queer art daddies: 'America I'm putting my queer shoulder to the wheel' (Ginsberg, 1956: 43).

A couple of months after our Valentine's Day performance, with all plans scuttled, all projects on hold indefinitely, & our collective future entombed in a state of perpetually suspended animation, I feel lost, disoriented, depressed.

Now, unexpectedly, Mark enters the Zoom call from stage left, in a dazzling spotlight. Indefatigable optimist & caretaker, he called a meeting with Judd & I to talk about getting back to work. I am despondent. How can we possibly work? How can we collaborate, how can we perform during a lockdown? Mark responds by borrowing a line from Lin Hixson, one of his art mothers: 'Are you making your work?' For the work must be made, the show must go on, we must continue to 'heed the call' like the firefighter who jumps into action as soon as she hears the alarm (Cecilia Vicuña told Judd & I that once over dinner).

These lines are the ancestral wisdom of our chosen art families, & over the past year, we learned that one must, indeed, continue to make one's work, that making work is a form of self-care necessary for survival, that collaboration is a mutual-aid network, & that we must never stop putting our queer shoulders to the wheel.

– Abraham Avnisan

References

Benjamin, W. (1969). Theses on the Philosophy of History. In: *Illuminations*, trans. H. Zohn, New York: Schocken Books. pp. 253–264.

Ginsberg, A. (1956). America. In: *Howl*. Intro by W. C. Williams, San Francisco: City Lights Books.

McCormick Bridgehouse & Chicago River Museum. (n.d.). 'Museum Exhibits.' Available at: http://www.bridgehousemuseum.org/museum-exhibits#:~:text=Known%20by%20early%20Europeans%20as,prevent%20beavers%20gnawing%20their%20trees. [accessed 25/05/2021].

II

Art in an emergency

"It's work"

5 *Here to Deliver*

Conversations with the ghosts of gig work

Shona Macnaughton

Shona Macnaughton is an independent artist based in Glasgow. Her practice is multi-disciplinary, including live performance, moving image, and writing. It explores the intersection of artistic, paid, and reproductive labour and the spatial politics of the workplace.

This chapter is an account of the re-making of a performance which took place six months after it was initially intended. Or rather, it is a comparison of two versions of the same performance, *Stout Hearted Heroes*, which was renamed *Here to Deliver*. In Summer 2019, I began a commissioned work for the University of Edinburgh's Contemporary Art Collection; in partnership with the Platforming Creativity project. I was to produce a new work responding to research undertaken on artists' engagement with the 'gig' and 'platform' economies. I developed the provisionally-titled *Stout Hearted Heroes*, where I would provide an unofficial taxi service for a forthcoming art festival. However, as the COVID-19 crisis developed, suddenly altering many aspects of our lives, the conditions upon which this proposed performance depended also changed dramatically. As gigs in the sense of live events were cancelled or moved online, so-called 'gig' economy occupations were transformed, and the role of digital platforms became more central to the circulation of goods, services, and creativity. The process of adapting this piece to digital technologies of circulation in the wake of the pandemic provides a case study through which to explore the entwinement of the artistic labour of performance and the wider gig economy.

There is a long running thread through my performance art practice exploring the interaction of artistic labour and other labour, for example, the durational performance and moving image work, *Adverts for the workplace = 48p* (2010), where I filmed myself in my cleaning job. This reflected the conditions of low paid zero-hour work,[1] but also the autonomy gained from filming my own exploitation, artistic labour

DOI: 10.4324/9781003165644-8

giving me the promise of future circulation. Importantly, this piece relied on the threat of an actual boss entering the forbidden filming scene. When considering my new commission, I decided to reflect on the shift to an entrepreneurial self which the gig and platform economies present; the lack of an accountable employer, the supposed autonomy, flexibility, and the internalisation of risk (Gregory, 2020). I sought to compare this with conditions of artistic labour. The new performance would examine the idea of freedom within capitalist relations, specifically, entrepreneurial capitalism playing to an individual's desire for freedom from traditional labour forms. I would relate this to the idea that art production can exist in a state of exception to this system, encapsulated in the idea of a 'labour of love'. In a similar method to my previous work, I would take up a gig economy job and make artwork from within that position. But as the commission began to take shape, I observed key practical differences between low paid zero hour and gig economy work. There was no downtime in the latter, no gaps in the structure of the shift which could be filmed or performed within. Furthermore, the gig economy relied on an individual's reputation in order to generate more work – for example, the star rating system, the opportunity for comments – and therefore needed the worker's full attention; in short, it was not possible to do both artistic labour and gig labour at the same time. This necessitated a twist in the concept: instead of performing from within a gig work occupation, I would devise a durational performance which mimicked the structure of the gig economy. The kind of circulation of reputation described above interested me as it seemed to correlate with structure of circulation that an artist is required to engage in: in general, there is a large amount of unremunerated labour which goes into a process whereby the artist speculates on their future value.

I focused on the creative economy of festivals as this provided a set of circumstances where artistic circulation directly interacted with gig economy platforms. Glasgow International, a contemporary art festival, was scheduled for the end of April 2020 and was, anecdotally, a time where the local art scene made heavy use of the platform Uber. Despite the awareness of its exploitative employment model, it is seen by festival audiences as a safe, easy to use app, particularly for visitors travelling around an unfamiliar city. I decided that I would offer an unofficial taxi during the festival, an act that was simultaneously a functional service and a performance. Money would not be exchanged for this service. Instead, the currency would be the passenger's agreement to be filmed by a dashboard camera. The footage from this would be used as part of a future artwork. In this value system, the audience/passenger would be transparently complicit in contributing to the speculative values of the future artwork. The final form of the moving image work would be determined by how much the audience was willing to participate. I would use the digital event ticketing platform Eventbrite, ubiquitous for art and cultural events, and a freely available tool. The performance would be booked like a live event, but it would be structured like gig economy work, my performance of work beholden to the customer/audience. I would be employed by the performance, on call at all times during the festival run of two weeks, my gigs/gig work deployed according to the circulations of people from venue to venue and how much the profile of the performance was able to increase. I imagined that, as the festival progressed, a kind of unofficial star rating system would emerge, as people learned through word of mouth that they could get a free ride in exchange for their participation.

Of course, in March 2020, the full reality of the pandemic hit the UK, and the systems of circulation on which this performance depended broke down. There was the cancellation of the festival, which took away the physical structure upon which it was based. But there were other subtle and no less significant alterations in behaviour which shifted the initial performance's ethical framework. I had spent the previous few months engaged in critical research around the gig economy's 'creeping individualisation' of labour (Webster, 2016). I had compared this seeming autonomy for the worker with the contradictory operations of digital platforms, who held 'exquisite control of the interactions they facilitate' (Calo and Rosenblat, 2017). I devised a work which had 'Uberised' my performance, using that model as a critical tool to examine artistic labour. Yet now these occupations were shifting in their significance in the public mood. The demand for some services such as Uber taxis or Airbnb travel accommodation collapsed, whilst other gig economy occupations such as couriers were relied upon for deliveries and they began to be redefined from 'low skilled' to key services (Gebriel, 2021). As April unfolded, major gig economy companies began to perform this role, controlling the narrative through their platforms, and reframing themselves as caring entities with moral imperatives. Uber, previously notorious for its aggressive commercial practices, marketed the non-use of its service as 'A company that moves people is asking you not to move' (www.uber.com, 2020). Deliveroo swapped 'The food you love delivered to your door' for the more servile 'Here to Deliver' (www.deliveroo.co.uk, 2020), and Airbnb offered free accommodation for key workers, offering the emotive aphorism 'We may be apart but we'll get through this together' (www.airbnb.co.uk, 2020). So what did this mean for my proposed performance? In a very short period, the precept of the straightforward critique of gig economy platforms itself was unmade, and concerns around autonomy in labour relations seemed less significant in an environment where employment in many arenas was precarious. Gig workers themselves faced a collapse in demand for their services and their position seemed even more uncertain. The kind of performance I had envisaged was untenable, as it depended on gigs. The normal circuit of both culture and labour was broken, and previous connections, theoretical, physical, and economic, could no longer be made in the same way. Any future work on this theme would have to undergo profound alteration.

The commission still had to be realised, however. I had been paid by the institution in 2019, and, in effect, I was in their debt. But I lacked a current source of income. As the months wore on, other work was cancelled, and with the emergency support for self-employed artists coming up short for several reasons, the most obvious way I could re-engage with the conceptual basis of the work was to become a delivery driver. I could provide a badly needed income for myself whilst researching post-COVID-19 working conditions. In July, I duly set about applying to be a Deliveroo driver. It seemed to start well. The Deliveroo website had an easy user interface, I uploaded the necessary documents, and I signed a weekend agreement agreeing to work at any time between Friday at 6 pm and Monday at 3:59 am. The anonymous Team Deliveroo seemed very positive, assuring me I was on the waiting list and that I would be contacted in due course, 'We anticipate particularly high demand over the next two months and, as a result, we are on-boarding additional riders to meet this specific increase in customer demand' (Deliveroo – come ride with us, 2020). I too was hopeful that I would be offered work soon. Every week I received emails 'checking in', assuring me that I was on the waiting list and I would be contacted once there were spaces available. Noticeably, they did not frame this as employment or as a job – instead, I was to wait for 'spaces' to become available. But as the weeks wore on, eating into the promised 'high demand' period, this prospect diminished. In August, I tweeted a picture of the weekly email alongside 'What's an artist to do when they can't even get the gig work to make artwork about gig work to make money from gig work because artwork about gig work money has ran out??' This was partly a joke at the expense of the artist desiring to be a mole in the machine, yet the machine had been taken away. But the fact was stark – this kind of work was in high demand and hard to come by – the idea of gig work supporting artwork was a ghost of its former self. In mid-September, the emails stopped coming altogether. During the past 15 years, casual work had become more precarious and less well paid, but it had never been so scarce. I, like many of my peers, was facing a situation where the (not ideal) symbiotic relationship of low-paid work propping up the low-paid or free labour of my art seemed, for the first time, no longer viable.

I now lacked the previous circulatory system of both the arts festival and its labour offshoot in the shape of the gig economy. Casual work had gone and, especially for the performance artist, circulation of work itself had become precarious. Even giving free or barely remunerated labour to performance would require searching for a new circulatory channel. Like many others, I still wanted to produce live performance. As this specific piece (*Stout Hearted Heroes*) related to a critique of concepts of entrepreneurial freedoms, which had now essentially disappeared, the new performance would have to adapt to the new conditions of labour and circulation. The performance would have to be part of a new service which was ethically permissible to receive, especially given the fact that even key services were putting bodies at risk. Even the title, *Stout Hearted Heroes*, which had ironically referenced the communist conception of the artist as worker, was now cloaked in an unavoidable layer of resonance. Key workers, now including gig workers, were presented in the media as 'heroes'. Artists or any occupation perceived as extraneous to survival were definitively devalued. I approached the servilely retitled *Here to Deliver* as the performance of a service that didn't exist anymore.

Instead of an 'in-person' taxi ride during the festival, I would offer a virtual experience of a taxi over the phone. This became a participatory audio piece. It included a narrative that was partly a memory of events which could no longer happen physically. In some ways, it became a memorial to pre-COVID-19 conditions and the deeply missed sociality experienced during gatherings such as art festivals. The aspect of circulation that did remain a feature of events under pandemic conditions was the use of social media, specifically, Eventbrite, which I had already planned to use in the first iteration of the performance. Now more than ever, it seemed that every seminar, talk, course, political meeting, or yoga class had to be booked through Eventbrite; indeed, it had become a central tool of the new artistic circulation. Without the physical adjunct of the venue, its aesthetic dominated, alongside Zoom grids, making every event seem to fold into one experience. Conceptualising the shift in what Eventbrite had become in relation to performance from physical to virtual, I considered the computer and its software as a mode of mediation, described as a series of levels and layers by which we experience culture in which crucially 'The complete syntactic and semantic rules of a computer language must be defined and written into any environment designed to interpret, parse or execute it' (Galloway, 2012). If we view computer mediation as layered and pre-written, we can see the obvious difficulty in providing the same level of live experience to an audience as was previously available. When moving from the physical to the virtual, the connection between bodies must be navigated by both performer and participant, through many different software and hardware which harbour their own rules. Eventbrite is one layer in a thick chain but has a particular function as a gateway, framing the beginning of many virtual experiences. Far from a neutral tool (the common metaphor is the marketplace, in this case, selling tickets to events) Eventbrite is inscribed with its own ideology and is an example of a highly artificial environment, of 'economies invisibly manipulated by operators and 'first movers' through algorithms and code' (Lovink, 2019). In other words, to provide a free one-to-one performance, you are operating *against* what the software was created for. To structure the event like a service was going further against its logic. The rules of one platform (Uber) were intervening in another (Eventbrite). This was difficult primarily because of the way in which the platform is structured for one-off events. For example, I had to create a series of events in one day with one ticket for each. I could only be available 'on call' in one-hour slots, as Eventbrite required time to be allocated in a certain way. It is set up for single events that last for a particular, pre-ordained amount of time – performance is thus conceived as having a beginning and an end. This hermetic allocation of time does not reflect the type of performance (of the working self) that Uber requires when logged on to their app. The number of gigs available is unknown to the worker until they have finished their shift. The control over their own working pattern stops as soon as they log on, when how much they earn is beholden to the algorithm's interpretation of the demand for the service. As a performer using Eventbrite, I could therefore only mimic the Uber platform to a certain extent. I could not be as fully flexible as the gig worker – if a ticket was cancelled, the platform did not automatically seek out new customers/audience members for me. I had more control over this platform than a gig worker has of, say, Uber or Deliveroo. Yet I still relied upon it in a way that, pre-pandemic, would not have been the case. Eventbrite and other social media shaped the way the performance circulated *and* was produced to a greater extent. Previously these platforms had mainly provided extra marketing tools, now they became where those works were primarily held, framed by their algorithms and particular aesthetics. Deliveroo riders have described themselves as uniquely powerful because they own their means of production – namely, their bikes – they can collectively simply stop working and the service is not provided (Cant, 2019). Indeed, there have been multiple actions brought on gig work companies and, in February 2021, the UK Supreme Court ruled that Uber were not, as they claimed, a mere booking agent, but were in fact employers and thus obliged to offer workers' rights accordingly (BBC News, 2021). Historically the perceived artist's autonomy has come from control over their work 'owning both the means of production and the product that she produces' (Beech, 2016). The shift to virtual and reliance on pre-existing platforms represents the performer (and the supporting institutional structures) losing some control over how their work is produced, yet lacking even a clear booking-agent-cum-employer to hold accountable.

It is clear that the speculative value system of the arts that is currently in place is extremely fragile, built on a framework of precarious and free labour which has crumbled away. Post-pandemic, the very idea of gig work and gigs was memorialised, what remained of them was a husk. During my performance, I would ask the question 'How do you make a living off what you do?', prompting the participant to remember how they would have answered pre-COVID-19. It was striking how many of those who identified as artists responded negatively, caught between the past and the present: 'I don't and I didn't before'. On top of the collapse of already-precarious freelance artistic work, often topped up by other zero-hour work, the performer faces constraints even in the circulation of their so called 'labour of love' and the narrow languages of platforms create a dissonance between performer and audience. *Here to Deliver* brought into sharp focus the peculiar mourning of these times; we feel the loss of what we once had, but we'd rather not have it back.

Note

1 'Zero-hours contract' is a term primarily used in the UK for a type of employment contract whereby the employer is not obliged to offer hours of work and the worker is not obliged to accept any work offered.

References

BBC News. (2021). Uber Drivers Are Workers Not Self-Employed, Supreme Court Rules. Available at: https://www.bbc.co.uk/news/business-56123668.

Beech, D. (2016). *Art and Value*. Chicago: Haymarket Books.

Calo, R. and Rosenblat, R. (2017). The Taking Economy: Uber, Information, and Power. *Columbia Law Review*, 117, pp. 1623–1690. DOI: 10.2139/ssrn.2929643.

Cant, C. (2019). *Riding for Deliveroo: Resistance in the New Economy.* Cambridge: Polity.

Galloway, A. R. (2012). *The Interface Effect.* Cambridge: Polity.

Gebriel, D. (2021). If You Don't Care What Happens to Gig Workers during Coronavirus, You Should – You're Next. *The Independent.* Available at: https://www.independent.co.uk/voices/coronavirus-deliveroo-uber-self-employed-gig-workers-sick-pay-a9430336.html.

Gregory, K. (2020). 'My Life Is More Valuable Than This': Understanding Risk among On-Demand Food Couriers in Edinburgh. *Work, Employment and Society*, 35(2), pp. 316–331. https://doi.org/10.1177/0950017020969593.

Lovink, G. (2019). *Sad By Design.* London: Pluto Press.

Webster, J. (2016). Microworkers of the Gig Economy. *New Labor Forum*, 25(3), pp. 56–64. https://doi.org/10.1177/1095796016661511.

6 Exploring Mars and other impossibilities

Liveness as labour

Marc Silberschatz

Dr Marc Silberschatz is the Head of Classical and Contemporary Text at the Royal Conservatoire of Scotland. As a director-researcher, he develops approaches to rehearsal, performance, and dramaturgy rooted in encounter between unconscious response and text. He holds a PhD from the University of St Andrews and the Royal Conservatoire of Scotland.

COVID-19 has prompted a sudden and radical shift in all areas of live performance. With theatres and other venues closed to preserve public health, artists whose normal mode of engagement with an audience is via live encounter have been forced to find new and different ways to rehearse, perform, and exhibit their work. As a director who has worked exclusively in the field of live (usually text-based) theatre for over 17 years and has no direct experience of digital performance, I find myself in a deeply unfamiliar landscape. While many artists have been working within a digital context for years, if not decades, this history and practice are far outside my own work and expertise. I cannot presume, therefore, to write with authority about this extensive, already extant lineage of digital performance. However, moving from live, co-present theatre to digital performance creates, arguably, a different context – one marked by a kind of creative grappling with new ways of thinking and making that endeavours to preserve something of the live, co-present theatrical context. This is the position from which I have been making work since the March 2020 lockdown and thus the perspective from which I write this chapter.

The theory and practice necessitated by this shift from the co-present to the digital is emerging through continual, sector-wide wrestling with both practical realities and theoretical and philosophical questions about what it means to make live performance in the age of COVID-19 and its aftermath. There is no surety, only uncertainty. For those who, like me, are making this digital turn for the first time, all

DOI: 10.4324/9781003165644-9

work might be considered work-in-progress, and this new digital ecosystem a laboratory, from which emerges my first experiment: *Mars Exploration: May 22, 1984*.

The focus of *Mars Exploration* was twofold. First, I was creatively interested in building a piece of work based on the de-classified transcript of an actual CIA experiment in remote viewing conducted in 1984 (United States Central Intelligence Agency 2000a, 2000b). Second and relatedly, the material presented the possibility of interrogating liveness, the apparent *sine qua non* of theatrical performance, in the absence of co-presence. Specifically, I aimed to explore whether liveness could be active rather than passive – something done rather than something that is. Further, I attempted to relocate liveness from the performer to the spectator. In *Mars Exploration* therefore, liveness (or a type of liveness) is found in spectatorial labour. This chapter considers the journey toward this formulation and its implications in more detail.

Throughout the lockdowns of 2020 and 2021, I have observed in many theatre-makers (myself included) a deep desire to preserve the live, immediate encounter theatre provides. Where our new, more isolated, and screen-based existence has made physical co-presence impossible, liveness is sought in the digital landscape through performances in which performers are doing their work in an ever-present and ephemeral now – through performances occurring in real time. This embrace of what Philip Auslander would call 'temporal co-presence' is both natural and straightforward given Auslander's argument that the advent of broadcast performance has already changed our understanding of liveness in such a way that 'temporal co-presence… is essential to the experience…whereas spatial co-presence…is non-essential' (2020: 296). And yet, if the transition to digital performance is considered only with reference to broadcast media and the conceptions it engenders, is something missed? Do we run the risk of addressing 21st-century challenges with 20th-century solutions?

Liveness as real-time performance rests on several assumptions that must be unpacked: In live performance, who or what is 'live'? The instinctive answer would likely be the performers and their work. But this privileges the perspective of the makers of the work rather than the spectators to it. Surely, they are more than passive. They are active co-participants. The question of where the art is located in live performance therefore becomes richer and more nuanced. The active participation of spectators suggests that the art extends itself beyond the real or virtual stage and exists beyond the boundaries created by the performers themselves. It is a kind of expansive liminality that creates different possibilities for understanding new potentials within the concept of liveness.

Being thrust into lockdown prompted me to reconsider these questions in relation to live, co-present performance and to consider them for the first time in relation to digital performance. In doing so, I was able to make *Mars Exploration,* a piece which had interested me for some time, but which I could not discover or devise a way to effectively stage in a theatre. From the reckoning – with both the material and the move to digital performance – that comprised the creation process, I offer provocations (but no firm conclusions) expressed by *Mars Exploration* about the nature of liveness in the digital domain, both for now and for when we are able to resume co-presence.

Mars Exploration: May 22, 1984, is a contradictory project. It is simultaneously fiction and nonfiction: a verbatim work that is also science fiction. It is a piece in which the text seems to tell a story: a person in a secure, closed location crosses vast spans of time and space to explore strange vistas and visions – if only in their own mind. Yet its narrative is deliberately difficult to parse: Who is this mind? Why are they undertaking this exploration in the first place? It prompts the viewer to see specific images and then frustrates imagining by presenting other, seemingly unrelated images in its visual montage. It strives for an intimate relationship with its audience while simultaneously holding them at a distance from what the work might mean. Finally, it is recorded and heavily edited, but (as noted above) attempts to offer the viewer a type of liveness.

This alternative liveness emerges first and foremost through its dramaturgy of disjunction, misalignment, and contradiction, making full use of the tripartite dramaturgical model articulated by director and performance expert Eugenio Barba (2010). Rather than defining dramaturgy as singular (which is how it is more conventionally considered), Barba proposes three dramaturgical levels present in every performance:

- the organic, which 'concerns the way of composing and interweaving the dynamisms, the rhythms and the physical and vocal actions of the actors'.
- the narrative which Barba defines as 'the interweaving of events which orientate the spectators about the meaning, or various meanings of the performance'.
- the evocative, 'the faculty of the performance to produce an intimate resonance within the spectator' (2010: 10).

It is the exploration of these levels and their interrelationship that shapes the form and content of a theatrical performance. Liveness considered as real-time, co-present performance can be located using this tripartite model. If we consider on which dramaturgical level this understanding of liveness is contingent, the obvious answer is the organic level. What occurs in and for the performers operates here. If liveness relates to what the performers do in the moment of performance, then it is a function of organic dramaturgy. This is, in effect, part of an epistemology of co-present performance. But does this epistemology translate if performance moves away from co-presence? When considering mediatised rather than live performance, Auslander has observed that 'mediatization is not just a question of the employment of media technology; it is also a matter of what might be called "media epistemology"' (2008: 36). If mediatising performance requires media epistemology, then is it possible that moving performance into digital spaces requires a digital epistemology? And if so, what might this be?

Mars Exploration's attempts to work with a digital epistemology began by changing the dramaturgical level on which liveness occurs. Rather than situating liveness on the organic level, *Mars Exploration* relocates it to the evocative level. In doing so, it places liveness within the spectator rather than the performer. It is not the labour of the performers that is live in *Mars Exploration*, but the labour the spectators are enjoined to undertake when viewing the piece.

Crucially, however, spectatorial labour is not alien to live performance. Kendall Walton argues that:

> In order to understand paintings, plays, films, and novels, we must look first at dolls, hobbyhorses, toy trucks, and teddy bears. The activities in which representational works of art are embedded and which give them their point are best seen as continuous with children's games of make-believe. Indeed, I advocate regarding these activities as games of make-believe themselves.
>
> (1993: 11)

Further, Walton argues that the actors, costumes, sets, props, arguably even the spoken text function as 'props' in games of make-believe each audience member plays (1993: 11). For Walton, the experience of a play occurs within the mind of each spectator because of the games they are prompted to play by what occurs on stage.[1]

An alternate framework to the conception of play centralises the notion of transportation. Through his examination of the cognitive processes of experiencing narrative,[2] Richard Gerrig deploys a metaphor of being transported to a narrative world in which 'the means of travel… are novels, anecdotes, movies, and so on' (1998: 12). Gerrig uses this metaphor because it reflects the self-described experiences of readers/viewers but argues that the apparent passivity of being transported masks a complex and highly active process for spectators (1998: 12–13). To extend Gerrig's metaphor, to experience a narrative world, spectators must act as co-constructors of a vehicle, which they then co-pilot in order to immerse themselves in the fiction.

Walton and Gerrig are concerned with broad categories of experience – representational art for Walton and narrative for Gerrig. By contrast, Dan Rebellato explores the nature of audience experience in live theatre specifically, analysing several models (including Walton's) and identifying their deficiencies (2009). Rebellato proposes his own paradigm in which 'when we see a piece of theatre we are invited to think of the fictional world through this particular representation. Theatrical representation is metaphorical' (2009: 25). Moreover, 'the means of theatrical production are metaphors for the worlds they represent' (Rebellato, 2009: 25). This model presents a demand for active engagement by the audience as the metaphor triggers a mental process by which the experience of the performance is shaped as we engage with and unpack the metaphor and its meaning(s).

Though different in their conceptions, each of these frameworks proposes and assumes a degree of audience labour. Spectators are working when they engage with live theatrical performance, whether that be through play, transportation, or the unpacking of metaphor. Given this, it is possible to consider Barba's evocative dramaturgy as a space that remains to some degree open, empowering each spectator to finish the work begun by writers, directors, ensembles, and creative teams. To interrogate the nature of that labour, Marie-Laure Ryan's articulation of different types of spectatorial engagement is useful. Ryan establishes two complementary forms: immersion within the work and interaction to shape the experience of the work from outside (2001). Both processes require labour from the spectator, but do so in different ways, with 'immersion…[as] the mode of reading of an embodied mind [and] interactivity/self-reflexivity [as] the experience of a pure mind that floats above all concrete worlds in the ethereal universe of semantic possibility' (Ryan, 2001: 354–355). These two poles of engagement are not mutually exclusive in a live theatrical context. The nature of audience labour will include elements of immersion and interactivity. For Gerrig, the audience's labour in transporting itself to the fictional world is largely immersive. The interactive elements are not directly connected to the performance but are found in the construction of the vehicle for immersion. For Walton, the audience's games suggest a greater degree of interactivity – the audience is prompted by the work to quite literally make or construct their own belief in something – though immersion is retained in the same way it might for people playing board or video games. Rebellato's model of metaphor arguably reduces immersion in favour of greater interaction, but this is less overt and focused on interpretation rather than co-creation. The ability to consider audience labour in live performance through the dual lenses of immersion and interactivity is profoundly useful as both are key features in the online experience.

This experience of immersion and interactivity is markedly different from live performance. When navigating an online space generally, individuals have the agency to shape and curate our experience. We choose where we 'go' online and what we do when we get 'there'. If I consider my own approach to online activity, it is usually marked by a shifting between multiple tabs and sites, combining information and experience at my own discretion.[3] In short, I construct my own journey through the online space – depending on the nature of that journey, one could even call it a narrative. I might immerse myself (as anyone who has ever found themselves in a 'Wikipedia loop' can recognise), but this immersion is a product of my agential, curatorial, interactive exploration of the digital landscape. Perhaps it is this instinct to curate and construct that makes sustaining focus on a single item in an online space so challenging. Doing so would surrender the power we normally have in this digital world – we would be submitting ourselves to being held in place rather than exploring freely.

By contrast, consent to being held in place is implicit when viewing a piece of live, co-present theatre. An audience's limited ability to control the viewing experience combined with a set of social and behaviour expectations creates conditions where being held is inevitable, and even desirable, as part of the immersive experience. Recognising this distinction, *Mars Exploration* concerns itself with finding a way to 'hold' its audience while satisfying the implicit expectation for interactivity the digital space creates. It attempts this through a different type of spectatorial labour than that engendered by live performance. It is transposed to fit this new space, returning us to the exploration of dramaturgical disjunction and contradiction and reconsideration of the relationship between spectator and material. Despite its nature as a recorded performance, *Mars Exploration* does not actually exist online or on the screen. In fact, it does not exist outside the subjective experiences of each individual spectator at all.

Indeed, it functions more like a guided meditation. A contradiction is introduced: where the mediated nature of *Mars Exploration* increases the distance between work and spectator, this positioning collapses the space into an intimacy that is manifested particularly in the actors' vocal performances, which draw on the theory and practice of triggering the autonomous sensory meridian response (ASMR) (Richard, 2018). Through this (and a corresponding use of directional sound), a second, related effect is achieved. The experience of performance is placed within the spectator's subjectivity. This is further heightened by the fact that much of the piece is written in the second person (one of the few editorial changes I made to the original transcript, which is written in the first person).[4] The performance resides not in the recording, but in the possibilities for what might occur inside the spectator. In a direct inversion of Ryan, the work immerses itself in the spectator rather than the reverse.

A counter-balancing interactivity was then required. Where some elements of *Mars Exploration* were engineered to create a feeling of closeness, others (specifically at the level of narrative dramaturgy) worked in opposition to this. In *Mars Exploration*, speaker and text are divorced from one another. At no point in the work do we see anyone physically utter the words we hear. All spoken text is therefore both diegetic (if considered in relation to the intimacy engendered) and non-diegetic (if considered in relation to the visual images). This is heightened by the source text's relationship to the visual imagery. The text is a description of things 'seen' during an actual remote viewing experiment, but (a few rare moments aside) the visual montage avoids direct illustration of what is seen by the remote viewer. Singular experience is eschewed in favour of multiple, parallel experiences.

There is more going on here than meets the eye or ear. These disjunctions between the narrative dramaturgy of the text and the evocative dramaturgy centralised in the piece operate as openings. Through these openings, a spectator can engage in a more interactive relationship with the work, seeking coherence to reconcile the apparent ruptures in immersion. A multi-level, web-like narrative is presented in which the story the remote viewer tells enmeshes itself with a story of an experiment, occurring in a closed lab on May 22, 1984. Both of these interweave with the exploration of an interiority – a psychic landscape or 'labyrinth of attitudes' (as quoted from James Baldwin in the piece's epigraph). While this discontinuity, disjunction and apparent randomness may at first glance suggest a simple collection of impressions or fleeting images, a narrative is constantly at play – one which dictated hundreds of choices made in working through the text and recording and editing the piece. The apparent disjunctions open the possibility of reconstructing this narrative or indeed constructing another one entirely. Labour is demanded. Spectators must sort and organise this material. They must recognise the clues (or clews) to assemble the experience into something coherent. The openness to interactivity means that an individual spectator identifying and experiencing the narrative we constructed to guide our choices in making the piece is likely an impossibility, but this is beside the point. Regardless of the degree of narrative shared between makers and spectators, the act of assembly creates liveness of a different sort. While the performers' work is not live, the spectators' is. Every viewing by every spectator is an occurrence – something that happens in the moment of viewing prompted by the labour undertaken by the spectator. It is a singular, ephemeral event engendered by, but separate from, the recording, existing only in memory. This description might just as easily apply to a pre-pandemic live performance. And yet, by opening ourselves to the idea that liveness is not limited to performers, but can include spectators, *Mars Exploration* makes a claim to liveness that is achieved through spectatorial labour. As Auslander suggests:

> It may be that we are at a point at which liveness can no longer be defined in terms of either the presence of living human beings before each other or physical and temporal relationships. The emerging definition of liveness may be built primarily around the audience's affective experience.
>
> (2008: 62)

To offer any further detail of the specifics of its narrative strategies and content would directly contradict its aim and purpose. The piece must be experienced. The labour it engenders must be undertaken. I therefore pass over any further detail in silence, leaving only an invitation to engage in the labour and to experience the attempt at liveness through a digital recording. Perhaps, this sounds improbable. But it is no less impossible than the exploration of the planet Mars in the year 1,000,000 B.C. while confined in a room somewhere in 1984.

Notes

1 I note here that Walton considers representational art generally, situating plays within that umbrella term. As I am concerned with theatre's move from a live to a digital space in this chapter, I limit my application of Walton's ideas to a theatrical context.

2 Narrative is also a more expansive term that includes a variety of art forms. Here I consider only narrative theatrical performance
3 I note here that I avoid social media – I can imagine that for the majority of internet users, this sense of curation is greater.
4 This uncommon form of address has gone unremarked in all conversation I have had with viewers about the piece, raising the question of whether this feature is noticed when the work is viewed.

References

Auslander, P. (2008). *Liveness: Performance in a Mediatized Culture.* London: Routledge.

Auslander, P. (2020). So Close and Yet so Far Away: The Proxemics of Liveness. In: M. Reason and A. M. Lindelof, ed., *Experiencing Liveness in Contemporary Performance: Interdisciplinary Perspectives.* London: Routledge. pp. 295–298.

Barba, E. (2010). *On Directing and Dramaturgy: Burning the House.* London; New York: Routledge.

Gerrig, R. J. (1998). *Experiencing Narrative Worlds: On the Psychological Activities of Reading.* Boulder: Westview Press.

Rebellato, D. (2009). When We Talk of Horses: Or, What Do We See When We See a Play. *Performance Research*, 14(1), pp. 17–28.

Richard, C. (2018). *Brain Tingles: The Secret to Triggering Autonomous Sensory Meridian Response for Improved, Sleep, Stress Relief, Head-to-Toe Euphoria.* New York: Adams Media.

Ryan, M. L. (2001). *Narrative as Virtual Reality: Immersion and Interactivity in Literature and Electronic Media.* Baltimore: Johns Hopkins University Press.

Silberschatz, M. (2020). *Mars Exploration: May 22, 1984* (captioned: https://youtu.be/0JBbOPqXNiE; uncaptioned: https://youtu.be/F0JpMJ31FmM)

United States Central Intelligence Agency. (2000a). Mars Exploration: May 22, 1984. CIA Freedom of Information Act Electronic Reading Room. Available at: https://www.cia.gov/library/readingroom/document/cia-rdp96-00788r001900760001-9 [accessed 20/07/2020].

United States Central Intelligence Agency. (2000b). Project Stargate. CIA Freedom of Information Act Electronic Reading Room. Available at: https://www.cia.gov/library/readingroom/document/cia-rdp96-00789r003300210001-2 [accessed 20/07/2020].

Walton, K. L. (1993). *Mimesis as Make-Believe: On the Foundations of the Representational Arts.* Cambridge: Harvard University Press.

7 Recorded performance as digital content

Perspectives from Fringe 2020

Chris Elsden, Diwen Yu, Benedetta Piccio, Ingi Helgason, Melissa Terras

Dr Chris Elsden is Chancellor's Fellow in Service Design at the Institute of Design Informatics, University of Edinburgh. This chapter was developed with support and collaboration across the AHRC Creative Informatics Cluster, with researchers and students in Human-Computer Interaction, Digital Humanities, Interaction Design and Events Management.

Introduction

As live venues closed throughout 2020, performers rushed to find ways to work remotely. From musicians and comedians to clowns and theatre-makers, live performance became digitally mediated, and by consequence, easily recorded and circulated online. As researchers, in 'Creative Informatics' we were curious about the emergence of recorded performance as online 'content' in a digital economy, and performers as 'content creators' (Brake, 2014). What did performers choose to record? How have they decided to distribute and control these recordings? What is their relationship to 'live' performances how could they record their work, without devaluing a live show (Bakhshi et al., 2010)? What, if any, are the 'creative transactions' (Elsden et al., 2021) and business models that can be built around this content?

To answer these questions, we conducted 20 in-depth interviews with participants who had planned to bring shows to the 2020 Edinburgh Festival Fringe, and spoke to them about their approaches to performing online. We identified ways in which artists experimented, innovated and most of all were *strategic* in the way they sought to use recordings of, and related to, their performances. Crucially, in the absence of live shows taking place, we describe innovations in recording that go beyond what is typically understood as 'live-to-digital' (Arts

DOI: 10.4324/9781003165644-10

Council, 2016, 2018) and illustrate how performance is rendered and transformed into digital content.

Research context and method

Our research took place in the absence of in-person performances at the Edinburgh Festivals in 2020, following this announcement on behalf of the five August festivals:

> For the first time in over 70 years, the five festivals that transform Edinburgh into the world's leading cultural destination every August are not going ahead this year due to concerns around the COVID-19 pandemic.
>
> (Edinburgh Festival Fringe Society News, April 2020)

Building on existing partnerships, our research focused on the Edinburgh Festival Fringe (or simply 'the Fringe'). As an open access and unjuried festival, shows were not formally cancelled or prevented from happening, although any purchased tickets and performers participation fees were refunded. Without specific direction from the Fringe Society, performers and audiences remained open to the possibility that some form of festivity may be possible in August. The diversity of the Edinburgh Fringe, in terms of genre, quality, professionalism, scale, audience, and internationalism (Frew and Ali-Knight, 2010; McCrone, 2019), offered a unique opportunity to understand how those working across the performing arts have responded to the pandemic and pivoted to work online.

Participant recruitment

We aimed to speak to people who had intended to participate in Fringe 2020 with a range of experience and roles, across genres. With support from the Fringe Society's Participant Services team to promote the study, we had more than 30 participants express interest in taking part and selected 20 of these, based on their background and availability. Participants are referred to pseudonymously throughout; most (15/20) were involved in some form of theatre; however, we also spoke to artists working in children's shows, improv, stand-up comedy, dance, puppetry and performance art reflecting the breadth of work performed at the Fringe. Our participants also spanned and had experience of many different roles in bringing a show to the Fringe (writer, director, performer, producer, marketer, stage manager, and curator). For some, 2020 would have been their first Fringe performance; others had brought work to the Fringe for more than 30 years.

Study protocol

Interviews took place over Zoom across August and September 2020. As semi-structured conversations, lasting around an hour, we probed participants on their practice, their shows, and how they had adapted (or not) to working in digital format. In concluding the interview, we also shared a series of 'Questionable Concepts' (Vines et al., 2012) about the future online landscape of the Fringe. For example, we asked about taking part in online competitions with other performers, an 'all-in ticket' that functioned as a festival pass for multiple shows, and geo-located digital content that could only be unlocked at certain locations in Edinburgh. During the interviews and through our analysis, the various roles of recorded content emerged as a core topic of discussion. In particular, we identified various strategies that performers described as they sought to generate value from recorded performance in new ways, within the limits of the resources, time and capabilities they had.

Recordings in progress

Initial concerns, barriers, and motivations to record

Our participants described several initial concerns and barriers to recording their work. First, many participants identified the need for high quality recording equipment and technical expertise, which could immediately distinguish or tarnish a piece of work.

> I spent… a good half an hour on [Fringe] Pick N Mix this morning and it is really obvious who has the decent recording equipment and who doesn't, and it instantly marks the quality of a piece and it may not be reflected in the content, but you instantly judge a piece when the recording is not of a good quality (Kelly, Theatre Director).

This technical challenge is directly related to a production budget and is exacerbated when recorded content was positioned in the context of home entertainment, as competing with easily accessible streaming platforms, such as Netflix or BBC iPlayer.

> It's a constant struggle, like, how do we as Fringe artists and Fringe creators produce something that is as the same standard as a Netflix special with 1,000 times less the budget? (Anton, Comic).

Similarly, a number of theatre-makers directly referenced the free distribution of *NT Live at Home* as setting a benchmark, especially for the recording of a whole play, which was out of reach for most productions, and raised unrealistic expectations about the quality and cost of digital theatre. Beyond technical quality, some performers had more fundamental concerns about the value of digitally mediated and recorded performance, especially where their work relied heavily on audience engagement, such as improv comedy:

> We've recorded little bits to try and get promo videos together, but we have always found it's something that translates with difficulty. It just doesn't seem as funny when you're not in the room and out of all context and the full kind of vibe around it. It is hard to capture it (Caroline, Improv Performer).

Other artists had a more fundamental opposition to recording where it seemed antithetical to their craft as performers. These comments reflected a common understanding around the unique experience of live performance in a shared time and space, but they also highlight how the subtleties of a particular performer's work, may not be easily translated for digital distribution.

> I've never recorded any of [my shows], and you have to watch them live, because I feel like our job as artists is to bring audiences together in real time (Paul, Performance Artist).

> What I have spent an entire career building up is an hour in my presence and I can't put that online in 60 seconds (Anton, Stand Up Comic).

For these artists especially, this time has been challenging, and their responses to the closure of venues have included stepping back entirely, taking part only in *live* online performances, taking on other events or performance roles, or trying to develop new work for the future.

> ...really it has been a hibernation year for us to kind of work out what do we do next. In some ways that's been amazing, because

> getting to stop and go how can we make our work more radical, how can we make our work more accessible? In other ways it's a loss of income, it's a loss of identity [...] It's been a challenge.
> (Emma, Theatre-Maker & Performer)

However, many participants were able to overcome these profound technical and creative challenges. Very few within the performing arts have the resources or opportunities to simply record a whole performance as 'Live-to-digital' (Arts Council England, 2016), especially without live audiences. So, what could they do? Undoubtedly, and perhaps unsurprisingly, there was a strong motivation to share and produce some kind of work to remain present and engaged with audiences and peers.

> Both as individual artists and also as producers of the company feeling like, because we've lost all of our outputs really and all of our performances basically overnight, that we lost ourselves and that we are basically nothing without that. And so, it was overcoming that and being, no, we're still here, we've still got our identity, we're still artists, we're still people (Simone, Producer).

> We've had to work fulltime through lockdown because we've got to pay the bills [...] we can't afford to sort of sit and do a lot of online free stuff, it's just a bit tricky. So yeah, it was... sort of wanting to be able to still create stuff but in the timeframe that we had (Arthur, Producer/Director).

At first, many venues and artists turned to archival content. Several participants regretted that they had not invested previously in recording their work, and 'realised how important it was' (Anton, Comic). Furthermore, many of those who had recorded some elements of their work previously – for example, to share with others in the industry – felt these recordings were rarely intended or suitable for wider audience consumption directly.

> ...obviously, anytime you make a show you make a film of it, like you just, you know, video the thing so that if a presenter can't come and see it... you can at least send them something [...] they're a good representation for somebody who really knows the artform, or they know what else they're missing and they can sort of make that leap. But for an ordinary audience member it's not great (Yvette, Producer).

Our participants hence described a variety of innovative responses to make the most of existing recordings, or to create new recorded work that they could share with audiences.

Seeking new forms of recorded performance

Throughout our interviews, participants were explicit about creating distinctive formats for recording, for example that could be more comfortably watched on a screen, and perhaps even as an accompaniment to viewing a live show. As one experienced theatre producer explained:

> The one thing we didn't want to do was just take the [film of a live show]. [...] What we wanted to do was to make something that really spoke (Yvette, Producer).

Likewise, several participants steered away from recording what might be understood as short films, and to try to find ways that highlight the unique aspects of a live performance, in new ways.

> ...if you want something that's beautifully cut and looks stunning, you might as well watch a film. I love film, and that's brilliant, but it's not...it's...you're not trying to recreate that medium, I think is the key (Kat, Marketer & Producer).

Examples of this 'third way' (Yvette, Producer); not quite film, nor theatre, involved recasting a dancer in a lead role, alongside a voice-over monologue; or re-staging a piece for a recording, then mixed with the audio from a live performance. Participants also felt that audiences could recognise and appreciate their efforts to innovate:

> I think it's when you are aware of the constraints on everyone you start to really appreciate how clever, for example, people recording music videos in their home and making quite a lot of stop motion comedy, just good fun. It is all, kind of, quite homemade, but I think that is the charm of it (Holly, Performer/Production Assistant).

In this way, by 'seeing people be creative with a new medium', performers were inspired to go beyond 'let's record it and stick it online' (Kelly, Writer/Director), in distributing recorded content.

Sharing the process, works in progress, and building online audiences

Considering how to make the most of recordings they did have, or could produce under the circumstances, several participants described ways to share their process and work-in-progress.

> We can't pull out of the vault that professional grade ready for distribution content, but what we do have is trailers, what we do have is fly on the wall bits and bobs of behind the scenes that we might have captured (Simone, Producer).

Participants also clearly had in mind the online contexts and social media through which their work could circulate. In Simone's case, her company were experimenting with Patreon, a paid subscription or patronage service, to manage how they shared this material, which had been curated alongside new interviews and reflections from the creative team.

> Why Patreon? ... we found that this whole promise of it being content, you know, we'll put content up if you join as a member, and actually that meant there was a motivation for us to continue making that content, as well. And, it also felt more like an artist's community rather than, like, a crowdfunder or anything like that, (Simone, Producer).

Their Patreon had been modestly successful so far, but would only be a small portion of the income required to sustain a small theatre company, especially in the wider precarious context of creative workers (Patrick and Elsden, 2020). However, beyond the opportunity to foster a core community of supporters around additional show material, this example illustrates how recordings of, through, and around a performance could become meaningful and valuable 'content' for an online audience.

Other theatre-makers also described strategically releasing a series of evocative clips, from rehearsals through to original 'backstage' content filmed to supplement the 'on-stage' storyline.

> On every day the show was meant to be on in [UK city], we posted out a different clip at that time, ...the longest was about five minutes, the shortest was about one minute... we saw that as a way of kind of getting interest (Aiden, Writer).

Importantly, while this was a response to being unable to perform, it has now become a strategy for building interest in future shows.

> Although it was borne out of necessity, it's been quite an interesting process [...]and it's given us a lot more different things, social media wise, that you realise can kind of add to the pre-show world (Aiden, Writer).

Another theatre company who had prepared behind the scenes style content to release through social media over the course of the Fringe festival described the approach 'as a kind of 50/50 of celebration, but also cheeky marketing' (Arthur, Theatre Producer). These approaches go beyond producing trailers, to expose the 'evolution' of a show, and mobilise all manner of existing and original recordings as a package of material to supplement a live theatre performance. As one comic suggested, a new part of his work as a performer will not only be 'trying to book spots, but trying to build content' (Anton, Comic).

Turning recordings into an event and events into a recording

Besides developing and sharing shorter form and supplementary content for social media, performers and producers discussed several ways in which recorded material could be embedded into live events. In the first instance, several participants sought ways to embed a sense of liveness into any online context.

> Look, if I'm going to show you my 45-minute video of my show, [...] I should be there live to introduce it, and then I should be there live at the end of it, to have some kind of something going on (Paul, Performance Artist).

In this way, even shows that were mostly or almost entirely made up of recorded content, could generate a sense of an event. Perhaps analogous to an artist preview or opening night, one company described running several 'watch parties' via video-conferencing platform Zoom, where an event would be built around watching a recording of a show together, with the opportunity to chat and discuss the show with the artists and performers. Acknowledging the recording itself is not comparable to the live show, this approach nonetheless creates a unique and live event, centred around the recording.

> We don't feel like it in any way replaces or really is a good substitute for live theatre ... but it's better than nothing, that was the attitude. Though we felt it was really important to still have a live element, especially as we weren't doing it free (Kat, Marketer and Producer).

Alternatively, we also heard from performers who were strategic in how they would generate recorded content from live events to subsequently distribute, closer to a traditional 'live-to-digital' model. Kyle, a puppeteer with a longstanding Fringe audience, managed to develop a live version of his stage show that he could perform relatively successfully over Zoom, charging a ticket price for access to the stream. Although he doesn't 'want to give too much of it away', as predominantly a sketch show he is able to clip material and post it to his YouTube channel. In addition, he shares an unlisted private YouTube link to the whole show for those who bought tickets.

> Meaning that only the people who have bought tickets for it are sent the link to watch the whole hour again. So they can share it with their friends, but they've bought that privilege. It would, I think, be self-defeating for me to, a couple of days later, put the whole thing out there online because they would just wait for that and feel a little robbed (Kyle, Performer/Puppeteer).

Longer term value of recording alongside live performance

Beyond understanding their practical and strategic approaches to engaging audiences with recorded performance, our participants discussed how they viewed the future role of recording. Recording can clearly give a show longevity, which it might not otherwise have, and shape one's portfolio.

> You'd have to have kind of the agreements with everyone of... how long it stays online, when it can get asked to take down, but yeah, again, I mean, it's that record, it's that history which helps for advertising yourself, for what you can add on your CV from it (Aiden, Writer).

Alternately, recordings can clearly also hold an educational value, or an opportunity to learn from peers, even in the context of improv, which was felt to translate poorly to a recording.

> For my students, I usually make them watch online shows, or shows that have been filmed and put online, I mean, from back in, like, 2013... And I have them watch that for their homework (Jake, Improv Performer).

In the specific context of the Fringe, we floated the idea of a 'highlights' package that could be generated from the increasing volume of recordings that could be made. Intriguingly, one producer argued: 'rather than it being a highlight of the Fringe, a better solution would be to commission it for February/March and, it is in development of what you will see at the Fringe. So, it's a taster' (Yvette, Producer). This framing speaks to the role that strategically recorded content can play in building anticipation and appreciation towards a live performance, rather than replacing or challenging it. Likewise, for Arthur, an emerging producer, it was important to make a distinction between a live and recorded run of a show.

> If I had a show filmed, I wouldn't release it until after it had finished. I think there's this nice element that if the show happens and then it goes on to screen, there's sort of this second wave or buzz, that people go, oh my gosh, I missed this show, or I need to see it (Arthur, Producer).

While film adaptations and digital broadcasts of performance are hardly new concepts (Erskine and Welsh (2000); Knapp and Morris [2011]), these examples highlight how the ubiquity and ease of recording video makes it possible, or even expected, that smaller independent shows produce some form of recording. What our participants emphasised however is the importance of being able to manage how recordings of their work are made available, to particular audiences, at particular times. Clearly, the business models for such recorded content may be rather different to traditional distribution of 'live to digital' shows.

Future recordings

Recording in service to live performance

Participants frequently highlighted to us fundamental differences between live and recorded performances, with the essence of live work at the heart of their craft, and something to be cherished and protected. This resonates with earlier research looking 'Beyond Live' (Bakhshi et al., 2010). For some, this was a reason to avoid recording; for others, it was an opportunity to make their art more accessible, shareable, and durable through recording, without undermining the integrity of a live performance. Clearly, throughout the pandemic, the desire to continue creating new work despite constraints has led to exploration of new mediums and formats for recording performance that extend both film and digital theatre.

We suggest the sector should explore what role venues and festivals can and should play in supporting artists in recording their work in these innovative ways, through the evolution of a piece, from conception, to rehearsal and through to performance on stage. Beyond simply recording whole shows directly in a venue – which is often expensive, and still a diminished product (Mueser and Vlachos, 2018) – venues might consider how to support artists in producing innovative, shorter form content, which can be used more flexibly throughout the lifetime of a show. Similarly, venues might consider innovative ways to distribute and share this content with their audiences, beyond trailers and social media clips. What if ticketholders could receive behind the scenes footage, or clues to a mystery on the day of an event? Or highlights of a monologue or song to relive on the journey home? Of course, this collaboration between artists, venues and festivals raises questions around who owns, licences and profits from these recordings, especially where significant investments or resources are provided by venues and festivals themselves (see also Berthold et al., 2018).

Opportunities, labour and value in building online audiences

Our participants showed a keen awareness to how recorded content could circulate through online platforms, and sought to be strategic in the way they released and presented their work. It was important to use recordings to build and engage audiences at the right moment, and over a sustained period. By tying in releases with planned festival activity, or packaging recordings as a monthly product for paying subscribers, participants sought to manage attention in an over-saturated media environment, as well as shining a focus on the core work of live performance that would take place on stage. While the use of social media marketing is commonplace (Hausmann and Poellman 2013; Miles, 2018), we have seen examples of particular forms of recording, exposing the workings and progress of a show, as ways to build online communities and support.

This implies a significant degree of platform labour to effectively distribute performance content through a range of social media and online communities. In a broader context of entrepreneurial and cultural work through social media, Duffy (2017) describes this often unpaid and overlooked work as 'aspirational labour'. Increasingly common across the cultural industries, what is striking from our study is the way that various kinds of traditional work in the performing arts can be creatively repurposed and rendered as valuable online *content* (Brake, 2014). Especially when apps such as TikTok, Instagram and Snapchat place powerful film-making tools into consumers hands, these clearly challenge more traditional approaches to recording performance. The examples described by our participants show creative work to negotiate this, developing distinctive and engaging content, with the resources they have, appropriate for shorter form media, which respect the artistic intentions of the original performance.

This ongoing translation of live performing arts into online content has wider implications than can be discussed here, in particular considering how performing arts become subject to algorithmic curation and power (Beer, 2017; Duffy, 2020). However, one specific concern that our participants sought to address was the value and 'creative transactions' (Elsden et al., 2021) that exist around this new work. On the one hand, much content was provided for free, or simply seen as promotional. Especially where content is repurposed, or work-in-progress, some felt it would unfair or even 'dishonest' to expect fans to pay for it. Others however found ways to bind recordings to paid, live experiences, or curate them as a product for paying subscribers. Looking forward, as performers have invested in recording their work in these new ways, we should explore the business models, practices and platforms required to make this work a sustainable and rewarding part of producing a live show.

Conclusions

Speaking to participants in Fringe 2020 about their experiences of pivoting online, what emerged was first: a realisation around the need and value for recorded content in engaging online audiences, and second; strategies for producing manageable and valuable forms of recording. We have highlighted various ways performers sought to preserve the value of 'liveness' and social events, and, especially in the hands of independent and smaller-budget productions, we distinguish these tactics from prior 'live-to-digital' approaches. Instead, we argue that in order to first engage, and then maintain digital audiences, performers have found themselves recast as 'content creators', navigating new digital economies. There are pragmatic lessons to be learned from our participants successes and failures in making the most from recording their work. However, more fundamentally, this work illuminates the need for further critical research on how live performance is rendered and understood as digital 'content', and the implications for those working in the performing arts as they become digital economies.

Acknowledgements

This research was supported by the AHRC Creative Informatics Project (AH/S002782/1), part of the Creative Industries Clusters Programme. We're grateful to our research partners at Edinburgh Festival Fringe Society who supported the study, and our interview participants for their time and candour.

References

Arts Council England. (2016). From Live to Digital: Understanding the Impact of Digital Developments in Theatre on Audiences, Production and Distribution. Available at: https://www.artscouncil.org.uk/publication/live-digital

Arts Council England. (2018). Live to Digital in the Arts Report. Available at: https://www.artscouncil.org.uk/publication/live-digital-arts-report

Bakhshi, H., Mateos-Garcia, J., & Throsby, D. (2010). Beyond Live: Digital Innovation in the Performing Arts. *NESTA*. Available at: https://media.nesta.org.uk/documents/beyond_live.pdf

Beer, D. (2017). The Social Power of Algorithms. *Information, Communication & Society*, 20(1), pp. 1–13. https://doi.org/10.1080/1369118X.2016.1216147.

Berthold, H., Grewar, M., Chillas, S., and Townley, B. (2018). Appropriating Value: On the Relationship between Business Models and Intellectual Property. In: A. E. L. Brown and C. Waelde, eds., *Research Handbook on Intellectual Property and Creative Industries*. Northampton: Edward Elgar Publishing.

Brake, D. R. (2014). Are We All Online Content Creators Now? Web 2.0 and Digital Divides. *Journal of Computer-Mediated Communication*, 19(3), pp. 591–609.

Duffy, B. E. (2017). *(Not) Getting Paid To Do What You Love: Gender, Social Media, and Aspirational Work*. New Haven: Yale University Press.

Duffy, B. E. (2020). Algorithmic Precarity in Cultural Work. *Communication and the Public*, 5(3–4), pp. 103–107. https://doi.org/10.1177/2057047320959855.

Elsden, C., Morgan, E., and Speed, C. (2021). Creative Transactions: Special Digital Monies in 'Break Kickstarter' Crowdfunding Campaigns. In: *Proceedings of CHI Conference on Human Factors in Computing Systems* (CHI '21). ACM, 13 pages. https://doi.org/10.1145/3411764.3445632.

Erskine, T. L., & Welsh, J. M. (2000). *Video Versions: Film Adaptations of Plays on Video: Film Adaptations of Plays on Video*. ABC-CLIO.

Frew, E. A. and Ali-Knight, J. (2010). Creating High and Low Art: Experimentation and Commercialization at Fringe Festivals. *Tourism Culture & Communication*, 10(3), pp. 231–245. https://doi.org/10.3727/109830410X12910355180982

Hausmann, A. and Poellmann, L. (2013). Using Social Media for Arts Marketing: Theoretical Analysis and Empirical Insights for Performing Arts Organizations. *International Review on Public and Nonprofit Marketing*, 10(2), pp. 143–161.

Knapp, R., and Morris, M. (2011). The filmed musical. In: R. Knapp, M. Morris and S. Wolf, eds., *Media and Performance in the Musical: An Oxford Handbook of the American Musical*. n. pg. https://doi.org/10.1093/oxfordhb/9780195385946.013.0011

McCrone, D. (2019). Treading Angels: Edinburgh and Its Festivals. *Scottish Affairs*, 28(3), pp. 290–317. https://doi.org/10.3366/scot.2019.0285

Miles, S. (2018). 'Do We Have LIFT-Off?' Social Media Marketing and Digital Performance at a British Arts Festival. *The Journal of Arts Management, Law, and Society*, 48(5), pp. 305–320.

Mueser, D. and Vlachos, P. (2018). Almost like Being There? A Conceptualisation of Live-Streaming Theatre. *International Journal of Event and Festival Management*, 9(2), pp. 183–203. DOI: 10.1108/IJEFM-05-2018-0030

Patrick, H. and Elsden, C. (2020). How Coronavirus Has Hit the UK's Creative Industries. *The Conversation*. Available at: https://theconversation.com/how-coronavirus-has-hit-the-uks-creative-industries-147396

Vines, J., Blythe, M., Lindsay, S., Dunphy, P., Monk, A., and Olivier, P. (2012). Questionable Concepts: Critique as Resource for Designing with Eighty Somethings. In *Proceedings of the SIGCHI Conference on Human Factors in Computing Systems*. pp. 1169–1178. https://doi.org/10.1145/2207676.2208567

III

Outreach and inclusion

8 'How we open the doors to a community'

Creative collaborations and aesthetic strategies in social isolation

Sarah Bartley in conversation with Anna Herrmann

Dr Sarah Bartley is a community arts practitioner and Lecturer in Performance at the University of Reading. Her work explores the intersections of participation and policy at play within socially engaged performance. In 2020, Sarah published her monograph *Performing Welfare: Applied Theatre, Unemployment, and Economies of Participation* with Palgrave Macmillan.

Globally, the pandemic has amplified existing structures of inequality with economically, socially, and racially disenfranchised communities disproportionately infected with, or dying from, COVID-19. Prison populations are acutely vulnerable to COVID-19 due to inhabiting persistently overcrowded and poorly ventilated environments. In a bid to prevent the spread of the virus, the UK Prison Service stopped family visits in March 2020 and people who were incarcerated regularly remained locked in their cells for between 22 and 23 hours a day. The isolation experienced by those held within the prison estate during this time was particularly acute.

Clean Break Theatre Company creates performance with, and advocates for, women with experience of the criminal justice system. The company's work includes a Members Programme at its site in London, a series of artistic projects run within the prison estate, and commissioning new work from women playwrights. In this interview with Joint Artistic Director of Clean Break Anna Herrmann, we explore how the company's programme was adapted in 2020 in response to the COVID-19 pandemic.

We talk about the relocation of the Members Programme online, alongside a discussion of 2 Metres Apart *and* Write 2 Connect, *two socially distanced projects delivered by the company that sought to establish or strengthen feelings of community and solidarity in Clean Break's creative work.* 2 Metres Apart *paired 12 artists with 12 Clean Break*

DOI: 10.4324/9781003165644-12

Member Artists to undertake eight weeks of creative collaboration. Write 2 Connect *was a letter-writing project that invited women from across the UK to send letters of hope and inspiration to women in prison and then encouraged the women in prison to write to Clean Break Members. In reflecting on these three strands of work, our conversation asks how commissioning practices that centre artistic collaboration and creative communities might resist experiences of social isolation.*

Concurrently, 2020 saw Clean Break reformulate two performances originally scheduled as stage productions: Chloë Moss' Sweatbox, *an immersive performance that takes place in a prison van; and Sonya Hale's* Blis-ta, *a duologue about homelessness, women, and sexuality. Subsequently,* Sweatbox *has been adapted for film and* Blist-a *for radio. Our conversation therefore also explores how the aesthetic strategies of participation in the pandemic might have led to an expanded range of forms being utilised by socially committed arts practitioners. What emerges across all the artistic work Clean Break delivered over the course of 2020 is an attention to care and community, and how this manifests in artistic practice at a distance.*

Could you start by sharing your experience of running a participatory programme for Clean Break Members during the pandemic?

The first thing that we did when the pandemic struck was a process of trying to firefight in a way, for all of our ambitions for 2020 as we all imagined it before March. From the outset we really prioritized our Members' needs, both in terms of support and in terms of engagement. We spent most of Easter redesigning the Members Programme as an online offer. It was completely new to us, I mean, digital has a role in our organisation, but it's never been a way that we engaged with our Members. As with many other organisations, we were having conversations about how we create a space online. What is the best way of engaging with a cohort of women who potentially weren't digitally native but also didn't have resources either? We did lots of emergency fundraising, so that women could have Chromebooks and data, so that our Members could access the programme.

We chose in that first instance not to do it with Zoom but to make these Vimeo offerings that women could do in their own way and time.[1] We maintained the model of our onsite programme and transferred it online with regular weekly Vimeos over the course of the Summer season. As we started feeling a bit clearer on the safeguarding issues around using Zoom, we peppered Zoom sessions in.[2]

Then, getting the building open again was a real priority in the Autumn. So, we invested a huge amount of time and resource to enable us to reopen safely and we were able to do that for the five weeks that we were on site. The Summer season was definitely about finding our feet with online delivery and then the Autumn season was about blended delivery. Then, when we went into that period of lockdown in December, we were able to just translate immediately into Zoom groups for the women. That was a good experience in terms of saying: okay, we can do this now. We've created a number of different pathways and the engagement's been really positive. So, it feels like we've now got that fluency to take forward.

Could you talk a bit more about those different models? I am interested in how you think experiences of participation shifted in Clean Break's work during this time.

Because geography was no longer an issue, who we've been able to reach and who we've been able to reconnect with has seen a major shift in our participation. We've always had an ambition that women who leave the programme still feel connected, but it's hard without an offer to sustain that. But this digital model has enabled us to reconnect with our wider membership in a brilliant way and because of that we've scheduled activity for them. So, we have this masterclass series – an additional layer of programming – for our wider membership. We have women that we haven't seen for ten years come back, and that's been really a good thing about the participation.

And some of the spaces I've been in, I feel really amazed at how much connectivity and togetherness there feels in these Zoom spaces. I think the women really want it and there's just a huge amount of generosity and openness, which creates this sense of a bond and a togetherness, regardless of the remoteness of it.

In many ways, there are lots of things that are positive, but I do feel impacted that there's something about not being in the building together and not sharing food together. Not passing people by and having informal conversations in the hallway, which is how we all connect. I do feel that's seriously lacking and there is a sadness associated with that.

And trying to invoke the care that normally happens in the space is what you've been hoping to gesture to by sending care packages to Members?

It's hard because what are the different ways of demonstrating care when you can't demonstrate it in the ways that we've been used to? So, things like the care packages have been a way of saying: we see you, we care about you, you're important, which would be what we're consistently wanting to communicate by how we interact with each other in the building. We have also set up a Creative Buddies project to buddy volunteers with Members who are particularly isolated. It's not about mental health support, but focuses on supporting engagement and creativity and working together, and writing something. So that was another way of trying to create that community that we were missing.

That idea of shared creativity threads throughout lots of the work that Clean Break have been doing during the pandemic, it really resonates with *2 Metres Apart* and *Write 2 Connect*.

Yeah, *2 Metres Apart* was about furthering our ambition of creating more collaborative ways of working with artists and Members. We designed something that we thought could offer a greater number of freelancers with employment and a lot of connection, but also advance that journey of what co-production and collaboration looks like for us. It felt exciting for Róisín [McBrinn] and I to be able to put *2 Metres Apart* together with quite a lot of freedom in it for those participating and with this ambition of not requiring a submission, just focusing on the collaboration, the connection, and the making. It was about building relationships and reducing isolation in that moment.

Then *Write 2 Connect* was really about feeling completely cut off from women in prison. There was no avenue to connect with them or with prisons in a way, because prisons were under such stress.[3] They were dealing with a huge challenge. We wanted to find a way of supporting women in prison, but not requiring prison resources, recognising that we weren't going to get such resources at that moment. But we were wanting to reach out to say: we see you, we are here. Our wider Clean Break community was wanting to, in some way, contribute. That enabled us to create *Write 2 Connect*, which was about calling out for women across the nation to write a message of hope to a woman in prison, and then inviting the women in prison to write their own messages back out to women in the community.

We worked with the organisation It's Not Your Birthday But and we wanted to make sure that it wasn't just a one-way process. Part of our values are about recognising that women in prison have as much to give – they are not just recipients of philanthropy, it's a mutual relationship. We got over 200 messages and artworks which we never anticipated – the invitation was to write a message, but people came back with the most extraordinary artwork. We sent that to our local women's prison, HMP Downview in Surrey, who distributed the all the letters. And then about 10% wrote back with messages that we then sent to our Members.

Alongside these two new projects you reworked Chloë Moss' *Sweatbox* from an immersive performance in a decommissioned prison van into a short film. Could you talk about how that felt as a director, especially working with a performance text so bound up with atmosphere and being immersed in an environment?

We were initially going to put *Sweatbox* to rest because by that point it had so many cancellations.[4] But I started thinking about what an amazing film it would be and whether that might be the way to ensure its legacy. We were fortunate with the timing and that Chloë Moss was on board to write the screenplay and the women were on board to do the filming. We got Quiet Storm, a film production company, to work with us and produced it as a short film. It was brilliant that we had the funding to do that, because the other thing that was playing on our minds was that we're not reaching audiences.[5] Our focus was on our Members and our artistic community, but how are we communicating with audiences? So, the creation of *Sweatbox* as a film was kind of centring that aspiration again.

One thing about *Sweatbox* was I knew the play because I'd just been directing it with the same cast, we knew it inside out and we knew what we could do with film that we couldn't do with theatre. That was exciting. You can go into the space that audiences can't, they can come into the van, but they can't go into the cell [in the van]. For me, as a beginner filmmaker, I felt really confident about what the film had to do. You had to see the sweat on the characters' lips. You had to feel the claustrophobia and intensity of the van. Then we got a great film producing company on board. It was exciting for me because the film set has so many different roles to theatre. The director of photography and the significance of that role in the creative process was really interesting. We worked with a brilliant director of photography, Sarah Dean, who captured beautiful, beautiful images. And then again, I didn't know what a creative role the editor has. I thought they delivered the storyboard that you've shared but Suga Suppiah, the editor, had a very creative input.

This shift, necessitated by the pandemic, feels like a real expansion of Clean Break's artistic practice to encompass new forms.

We'd been conscious of wanting to extend our digital voice within our artistic work and trying to find ways of weaving it in, but the pandemic absolutely fast-forwarded that. And there's a lot of joy in that. Personally, making *Sweatbox* was a fantastic experience because it was exciting learning. It's venturing into new territory and has felt very different, but equally really joyful. I think Róisín felt the same about creating an audio play. What's also new for us is considering what the right routes to the audience are for these pieces of work? There are many options, and we are considering the best ones for us. It's been a steep learning curve, but we won't go back – digital approaches will become part of our repertoire and our voice for the future.

Could you say a little more about *Blis-ta*, the audio play that Róisín directed at the end of 2020?

That was part of thinking about how we're going to produce our work differently. We had been making plans to produce *Blis-ta* in a theatre in early 2021, before the pandemic, but we realised that it wasn't going to be possible. Then spurred on by, the playwright, Sonya Hale's, ill health at the time – and really wanting her to know in her lifetime that her work was being produced – we decided to just make it. Sonya was really excited by radio and the idea of it being an audio play, so Róisín set about doing that and we had great support. The National [Theatre of Great Britain] gave us their studios to do the recording. You know, it felt quite supported by our industry to enable us to make that happen.

That idea of support across the industry feels really urgent, I wonder if you could speak about the importance of collaboration in Clean Break's artistic commissioning practices during the social isolation of 2020?

I suppose *2 Meters Apart* is the clearest example of a project in which we were looking to further our investment in collaboration, which is in a way a follow up to *Inside Bitch*, the project that launched our new model in 2019. *Inside Bitch* was created by Stacey Gregg and Deborah Pearson, two professional artists, alongside four of our Member Artists with lived experience of prison. They worked together to co-create a production. We still have other commissioning pathways with more of a traditional writer model and a number of writers in our cohort on their journey of creating their plays, but we wanted to explore further ways Members would work with artists as equals.

There's nothing to specifically produce at the moment, but it's the relationship of collaboration and co-production that we're investing in. It might result in something and it might not. But we'll ensure that within our body of potential commissions we've got these different ways of working that aren't necessarily about autobiography – it means that artists and Member Artists are equal partners in the creation of the work. It's interesting to hear you articulate the thread of collaboration, it very much predates the pandemic, but then in that moment of social isolation, there was a clear understanding of where you might turn to or invite this collaboration to continue.

Some of the *2 Metres Apart* Artists have talked about how lots of theatres at the start of the pandemic were commissioning *work* and really wanting to put work out. There was something distinctive about Clean Break's offer to invest in a collaboration over an output-driven model.

I mean, we did have an imperative to reach audiences but, because of our social mission, we weren't compelled in the same way as producing theatres, who were suddenly not able to communicate with audiences. We have different ways of talking to people that didn't require us to produce theatre, which is something that we've been developing over the past few years around how do we talk to audiences outside of our shows. We've been able to host online events that kept the concerns of women and women's lives on the agenda.

Do you think that the advocacy work that Clean Break does changed during the pandemic?

I think it's definitely given us more confidence. It's in the DNA of Clean Break because of the founders. That's who they were from start. But we have struggled at different points around identifying what our contribution to campaigning is because there's Women in Prison, Howard League for Penal Reform, the Prison Reform Trust, who specialise in this. Theatre is what we know and that's what's unique about us, but then how does that support our campaigning? But this year, I think particularly with the digital nature of being able to host online events and with the success of our events programme and in our anniversary year, we've grown in ambition.

One of the things that has happened during the pandemic is that, nationally, women's organisations in criminal justice have created regular check-ins for mutual support and shared responses to all the issues that they're facing. We've been on the periphery, but it has produced a coordinated national voice and an ease with working together. This ease and familiarity were really helpful when we approached Birth Companions to join us for our International Women's Day online event on maternal imprisonment, which was a huge success. And the need for campaigning now, I mean, it's never not been there, but it feels so present and it feels like we have to be part of that collective. We will carry on doing digital events beyond the pandemic. It's one of the legacies that I hope will be really strong.

Are there other legacies this period has left, or other ways your practice as a company has been shifted or reoriented during the pandemic?

Definitely embracing the digital and how we move forward with practices of collaboration. That was definitely part of our mission before the pandemic but it's come into sharper focus. In terms of our organisational culture, what we have put energy in this year is around the wellbeing and care of our staff. Also, the anti-racism work that we started, the mistakes that we've made over it, and the need to restart with our team at the very heart of that work has been significant. Conversations about company culture, collaborative decision-making and the desire to engage more with our Members across all areas of company life, that whole piece of work has sharpened this year. It was work that we wanted to do, but it was more on the periphery, and it has definitely been centred this year out of need and it will carry on being the centre. Beyond that, we're more actively thinking about opening our door. Not just thinking about our Clean Break community but, as the world recovers from the pandemic, about who else we could include and how we open the doors to a community without geographical boundaries.

Sitting at the intersection of two sectors severely affected by COVID-19 – culture and criminal justice – Clean Break's turn to collaboration and co-creation resonates with a broader reorientation of the social in performance practice during 2020. Amidst the acute isolation resulting from the pandemic, the company turned to an aesthetics of collaboration that centred artistic relationships and creative exchanges. This resisted the impetus to produce performance and instead placed value in community dialogues – between artists and Member Artists, volunteers and Members, and women in the community and incarcerated women – creating new models of social practice that responded to the interpersonal absence brought about by the pandemic. Concurrently, this investment in co-creation utilised new forms of creative practice (digital, radio, and film) to navigate the terrain of social distancing, platform the communities they work with, and expand the reach of their stories. Clean Break sought to find ways to underpin this ambition with care for the Members, prison, and artistic communities they engage. In a year that reasserted the value of care work, artists responded with a proliferation of new ways in which care might be cultivated within arts practice.

Notes

1 Zoom offered a live space for interactive workshops; while Vimeo was used to create asynchronous material recorded by practitioners.
2 The use of asynchronous Vimeo sessions also enabled Clean Break to open up their Members programme to women's sector organisations across the country for the Summer season.
3 You can learn more about the COVID 19 crisis within women's prisons in the UK on the Women in Prison website: https://www.womeninprison.org.uk/campaigns/take-action
4 *Sweatbox* was originally produced in 2015 and restaged in 2019 and 2020. The performance takes place in a decommissioned prison van with performers occupying the three cells and audience watching from inside the van. The production was due to tour to ten UK universities in early 2020 but was impacted by the UCU industrial action and then the pandemic.
5 The *Sweatbox* film was supported by the Arts and Humanities Research Council project: *Clean Break: Women, Theatre, Organisation and the Criminal Justice System* led by Caoimhe McAvinchey, Deborah Dean, Anne-Marie Green, and Sarah Bartley.

9 Mediating experience

Online community arts participation, a postphenomenological framing

Rebecca Stancliffe

Rebecca Stancliffe is a Postdoctoral Research Fellow at Trinity Laban Conservatoire of Music and Dance and investigates the impact of the institution's diverse participatory programmes. She is also a lecturer in dance technique and contextual studies at Trinity Laban. Rebecca's research interests include dance analysis and documentation, and digital studies.

Introduction

During the COVID-19 pandemic, performing arts activities moved from studios and practice rooms into people's homes with the adoption of video conferencing platforms. Tools such as Zoom are not 'merely functional and instrumental objects, but [...] mediators of human experiences and practices' (Rosenberger and Verbeek, 2015: 9). In other words, Zoom not only circumnavigates the inability to meet in person but reorganises performing arts delivery and engagement. This chapter examines the lived experience of online community singing and dance participation during the pandemic. Adopting a postphenomenological lens, and triangulating data from participant observation, 'interviewing objects' (Adams and Thompson, 2011), and semi-structured interviews, I explore how digital media transforms experience with particular reference to spatiality, social impact, and group singing. I focus on two community groups: an older adult's voice and movement class and an arts and health singing programme. Each group met in person on a weekly basis prior to the pandemic and now participate online.

DOI: 10.4324/9781003165644-13

Methodological framing

Postphenomenology is an interrelational ontology that examines human-technology relations (Ihde, 2015; Rosenberger and Verbeek, 2015). The empirical methodology analyses the roles and implications of technology in constructing experiences and practices (Rosenberger and Verbeek, 2015: 31). To examine the impact of shifting to online delivery for community arts, I draw from what Don Ihde refers to as *embodiment relations* which focuses on how technologies 'transform a user's actionable and perceptual engagement with the world' (Rosenberger and Verbeek, 2015: 14; see Ihde, 1990).

Digital media, which includes digital content, tools, and personal devices are at the front and centre of online engagement. As Robert Rosenberger and Peter-Paul Verbeek suggest, 'When a technology is "embodied," a user's experience is shaped *through* the device, with the device itself in some ways taken into the user's bodily awareness' (2015: 14 [original emphasis]). Subsequently, technologies are not neutral and, according to Ihde, have 'a magnification/reduction structure' (Rosenberger and Verbeek, 2015: 16). This means that

> through the mediation of a technology, we not only receive the desired change in our abilities, but always also receive other changes, some of them taking on the quality of "tradeoffs," a decrease of a sense, or area of focus, or a layer of context.
>
> (Rosenberger and Verbeek, 2015: 16)

The online delivery of community arts during the COVID-19 pandemic made it possible for people to sing and dance together during national lockdowns. Extending participation in this way (a change in ability or magnification) employs different body skills (both desirable and trade-offs) and exerts communicative limitations (reductions) that co-constitute experience. Such magnifications and reductions are the focus of this chapter. I describe how screen orientation, enveloped into the participant's awareness, diminishes the experience of spatiality, while on-screen representations of the self captured by the device's camera can act as a feedback mechanism in movement tasks. Zoom mediates social interaction, yet sound latency (a trade-off) alters the experience of communication by disrupting conversational flow and renders community singing virtually impossible. To mitigate losing the collective sense of togetherness, I explore how accommodations such as *artificial choirs* seek to replicate activities like singing in the round.

In Summer 2020, three community arts groups at Trinity Laban Conservatoire of Music and Dance were invited to reflect upon their experience of remote participation as a result of the COVID-19 pandemic. Evaluation findings from online focus groups and questionnaires were subsequently used to shape online provision. Furthermore, I used emergent themes to inform the development of a research project that examines how online delivery transforms practice and engagement in music and dance.

Participants from two community groups consented to taking part in this research. The first group merges vocal and movement improvisatory techniques and creative expression to explore major themes affecting participants' lives. The second is an arts and health singing programme for individuals with long-term chronic lung conditions such as asthma, chronic obstructive pulmonary disease (COPD), and pulmonary fibrosis. Adopting a non-medicalised approach, the class is designed to help manage feelings of breathlessness whilst taking part in a fun, social activity. Both groups met in person on a weekly basis prior to the pandemic and now meet online. However, not all group members made the transition to remote delivery because they do not have access to digital media or are resistant to online participation. Newsletters, creative postal packs and phone calls allowed facilitators to stay in touch with those individuals, but such exclusions necessitate further consideration for ongoing and future community arts provision.

In exploring the shift to online delivery, I was involved with the groups as a participant observer on a bi-weekly basis. This ethnographic method (Moustakas, 1994) offered first-hand experience of remote delivery, helped to understand the online setting and learn more about the context of participation. My field notes and reflective accounts generated data about the meaning of participation and were used to contextualise the experiences that participants identified as meaningful.

On alternate weeks, I 'interviewed objects', a method that positions technology as important qualitative research participants and 'attempt[s] to better understand how digital things [...] inform but also deform, conform, or transform practice' (Adams and Thompson, 2016: 89). Employing techniques such as 'listening for the invitational quality of things' (Adams and Thompson, 2016), I 'interviewed' the digital media involved in online singing and dance activity to understand how they shape actions, gestures, and perception.

During the three-month research, I conducted 12 semi-structured interviews on Zoom to gain insight into the older adults' lived experience of community arts remote delivery. The descriptions that arose in these interviews are triangulated with the data from participant observation and interviewing objects.

The screen and spatiality

Online, participants are united in a virtual world, instead of coming together in a physical space designated for group activity. They are technologically connected, yet spatio-temporally distributed, and the distinction between public and private space is erased as they spill into each other's homes. For some, a loss of *eventness* characterises this altered delivery as the effort to reach in-person sessions is part of their routine, an opportunity to exercise and warm up before class. While, as one participant says, 'in some ways it's a lot easier just to walk downstairs and sit in front of the computer [...] I'd much rather be battling the rain and the wind and standing on the station, catching the train'. Remote participation, another explains, means 'we haven't gone anywhere [...] we're all spending half our lives slumped over the computer'.

In a postphenomenological case study, Stacey O'Neal Irwin describes the spatial orientation towards our devices:

> I view the screen in a forward stance [...] Many technology users say they "sit in front of" the screen [...] For me, to be in front of the computer is to face this kind of spatial arrangement and orientation [...] Without looking at the screen, I could not view the digital world.
>
> (2016: 51)

Irwin asks, 'Is the front of the digital media where the body stops while the mind is engaged within the computer?' (2016: 51). Encouraged by the positioning of the device, often on a table or desk for access and visibility, the invitation to sit during online activities is compelling, and more so for singing than for movement tasks. Recognising a desire to combat inactivity (a trade-off), interviewees reflected that they were frequently invited to stand and, for the arts and health singing group, there was a greater attention to warming up the body at the start of class.

Irwin suggests that the 'habit of orientation [...] through the screen is a constant negotiation of lived space' (2016: 51). At home, participants often move in smaller spaces than is the case for in-person classes, which is reflected in movement content. Instead of 'running around the room' in improvisation, as one participant describes, movement becomes less expansive on Zoom. One participant likened their spatial experience to Pilates in the sense that its use of general space is restricted, while another suggested that Zoom might be more appropriate for fitness classes than creative movement. When the screen becomes the portal or frame of participation, bringing awareness to one's surroundings and the three-dimensional world becomes important. In both groups, participants are encouraged by class facilitators to bring awareness to the three-dimensionality of the breath and the body, to fully inhabit their lived space. Nevertheless, there is a trade-off: as actions are learned from and oriented towards the screen, the spaciousness of movement is diminished. The screen-lifeworld shapes choices and transforms bodily actions, constructing a perceptual experience that is different to the studio-lifeworld.

Participant observation led me to reflect on the image-body as other: a technological projection of one's body as an onscreen object. 'As phenomenological literature has long shown', Ihde notes, 'one can simultaneously experience one's here-body from its core while having a partial, but only partial, "external" perception. I can see my hands, feet, part of my frontal visible body from the focal point of my vision' (2002: 6). On Zoom, if *hide self-view* is not selected, the here-body is reflected back to the participant as an image-body, one amongst others in a gallery of moving images. Interviewees drew parallels between this and the experience of working with dance studio mirrors, using the image-body as a feedback mechanism to monitor and modify the timing of unison movement phrases, for example. The screen image-body integrates into the here-body experience.

Moving together online necessitates a different kind of seeing to the peripheral vision employed during in-person sessions. Seeing others is reduced to the two-dimensional image-body captured on camera and represented on screen. These representations are often partial owing to the lack of depth in participants' physical spaces, as well as needing to be close to the screen for visibility. Online engagement thus involves negotiating both *seeing* and *being seen*, which encourages diminished spatiality.

Social interaction

While mediating face to face communication, social interaction on Zoom is described by one interviewee as 'much better than nothing [...] but it is a compromise', a consensus shared by others. One participant reflects that:

> the sense of community, the sense of support, it was quite an emotional experience being there [in person], very powerful at the time. You don't quite get that on Zoom, not being in the room. There is a little bit of it, but it's not the same.

Interviewees speak about having glimpses of prior experience, fleeting moments where they recall the emotional and energetic connection of the group, of 'what it was like [...], how it used to be to work together'. This group dynamic established prior to the pandemic is attributed, in part, to the success of online classes, but also engenders a sense of loss. Personally, having worked extensively with one of the groups, I miss a participant's gentle teasing when catching me yawn as an effect of exercising my lungs, the group's triumph of mastering a new song, and the laughter erupting from a new comical warm-up. Nevertheless, the online substitute is important for maintaining group interaction. For individuals that live alone, the class is the first time they have spoken to someone that day, or even for several days. Participation, one person explains, is 'not just about the breathing exercises [...] there are other stuff that attaches to that session':

> it's good to see familiar faces in the breakout rooms, which are of course chatty. I mean, everyone is saying "good to see you," "it's nice to see you," and it's a little chat about what they've been up to and what we're all experiencing.

Remote delivery also offers structure at a time when many participants are retired, or shielding:

> we lack structure and routine [...] there is now absolutely no difference between a weekday and weekend. So, you know, every day is the same and most of us [...] can't remember, haven't got a clue how we account for our time. We just get so slow, and we sort of drift from one time to the next [...] It's a strange situation.

Acknowledging the social impact of the sessions, time to catch up with others is integrated into the class structure. Breakout rooms at the start of each session are, one participant says, 'brilliant as a substitute for the getting there early and chatting before the class begins'. Described as 'democratic' and 'levelling' where everyone is welcome, this space 'helps maintain the group interaction [...] they're not a throw away, they are an important part of the session'.

However, being 'thrown together in a random selection of people' when breakout rooms are assigned met with mixed reactions. One interviewee recalls their in-person experience:

> I'm casting my mind back to this time last year [February 2020], when we were actually going to the [venue…] You could chat in little groups or you could chat with one other person. You were able to not necessarily *choose* who you spoke to, but it was much more spontaneous and much more organic, the conversations.

The same participant notes that, 'For the first two terms [online], I did not get to speak to several people who I would have loved to have spoken [with]'. For others, breakout rooms are 'in some ways, even better [than the in-person equivalent] because you're just thrown together'. One participant described being in a breakout room with 'somebody who joined the class in person just before lockdown' who has since

> become a really, really good friend, which just wouldn't have happened if we hadn't had breakout rooms […] There's a kind of intimacy about it, which probably wouldn't have happened if we'd been in person. It would have seemed too soon to contact each other and say, "let's do something".

Zoom disrupts habits of social interaction by restructuring the group dynamic. Eliminating choice in who to socialise with means that participants are encouraged to speak to different people. This change results in an inclusivity that is valuable for newer group members, although maintaining established relationships may be conceded.

Scheduled social spaces brings participants together for meaningful conversations, but also helps to mitigate the challenges that come about through the disruption to conversational flow. Anne Friedberg (2006: 93 cited in Irwin, 2016: 55) who explores metaphors of the screen explains that 'The moving image (of frames) produces a complex and fractured representation of space and time. And once two or more moving images are included within a single frame […] an even more fractured spatiotemporal representational system emerges'. Zoom's latency combined with simultaneous conversation results in fragmented and clashing sounds, and the bigger the group, the greater the challenge. Becoming accustomed to new technology and this fractured experience is part of Zoom engagement. In the beginning, when classes first moved online, one participant observed,

> There were quite a lot of technical hitches [...], understandably. It was new to everyone. The issue with people over-talking... it's very difficult to say your piece sometimes. Then, if you start talking at the same time as someone else... You both back down and then... You lose the thread of the conversation, it becomes a bit disjointed.

Disruptions to natural conversational flow have been keenly felt yet accepted as part of the experience. To minimise disruption, participants modify their behaviour. For example, one interviewee describes looking for 'which square is going to light up [on Zoom to highlight the speaker... so] you don't get the conflict between who's speaking'. Further developments in Zoom etiquette include monitoring one's contribution to the group. A participant reports 'mak[ing] a deliberate effort [...] to shut up and let other people get a word in edgeways' while another comes to the session prepared with conversation starters. Exaggerated forms of non-verbal communication have also been adopted, such as vigorous head-nodding or enthusiastic thumbs up to signify agreement.

While some are liberated by what they experience to be a 'less inhibiting' space making them 'a bigger personality online than I am [in person]', others are conscious of contributing less than before:

> I don't participate verbally as much as I would have done in the room. It's not so easy to do that [...] It's difficult. When you're in a room, it is possible for more than one person to speak, isn't it?

Another participant reflected that their in-person persona is no longer possible: 'it's a whole routine that I've been practising for months but I'm unable to do on Zoom'. As participant observer, I have become aware of the extent to which the virtual space encourages different levels of participation. While discrete conversations during in-person classes are possible, an individual's contribution on Zoom is directed to everyone. The exchange is more explicit, and individuals can appear more confident or forthcoming online. This suggests that impressions of identity and selfhood are constructed differently in the virtual space.

Singing together

The difficulties of online communication extend to singing together, an obstacle experienced by both groups. Participants are muted for much of the group session to minimise distraction from latency and audio feedback. When singing, only the facilitator is unmuted which minimises disruption to sound quality and focuses attention on the activity in hand. One participant was keen to point out that

> there isn't a feeling of they're the teachers and we've got to all be quiet [on Zoom]. And obviously [verbal input from the group has] got to be limited otherwise [the facilitators] can't get the words out [...] But occasional bits of banter are acceptable.

The facilitators make space for suggestions and insights from group members who are invited to unmute between songs and tasks, generating exchange characteristic of community arts.

Singing on mute can be a liberating experience as, for some, it gives licence to deviate from the harmony set by the facilitator, sing with more gusto, and worry less about how they sound. But on the whole, being muted is described as a loss, as one participant explains:

> One always felt supported by everybody [when singing in person]. There was a great spirit of support [...] I didn't worry about singing out of tune or whatever [...] I find that if I'm in a small group singing, then I'm supported by the voices on either side of me, because I'm not a strong singer.

Rather than hearing (and being part of) the ten or fifteen other vocals, participants hear only themselves and the facilitator singing. Muted group singing effectively results in multiple duets performed simultaneously. Yet these duets are unidirectional: participants sing with the facilitator, who in turn performs solo because they are the only ones unmuted in the virtual space. While the in-person experience generates a sense of togetherness, singing alone can heighten self-consciousness, especially if one is singing in earshot of others at home. *Artificial choirs* where layers of vocals are pre-recorded for the group to sing to appear to mitigate the isolation of singing alone. While, as one interviewee explains, 'It will never replace being in the room [...] The voice part is quite challenging', vocal layering is a 'good-enough' work around, as a temporary solution.

Conclusion

'Postphenomenology is the practical study of the relations between humans and technologies, from which human subjectivities emerge, as well as meaningful worlds' (Rosenberger and Verbeek, 2015: 12). Through this lens, technology is revealed as neither secondary nor epiphenomenal but that it '*non-neutrally* [...] transform[s] experience' (Ihde, 2015: xi, xii [emphasis in original]). In describing perceptions of space, social interaction, and singing it becomes possible to see how community arts engagement is shaped through Zoom.

Differences between in-person and online delivery are reflected in the qualities and structures of participants' experience. Ihde suggests that the 'audiovisual has become deeply sedimented in our seeing/hearing and is taken for granted in our experience' (2002: 8), but there are degrees of transparencies in which 'a device (or an aspect of that device) fades into the background of a user's awareness as it is used' (Rosenberger and Verbeek, 2015: 14). My research suggests that transparency in community arts participation depends on the nature of the activity. For instance, while latency disrupts conversational flow, breakout rooms, one participant suggests, makes it feel 'like we're in a sitting room somewhere having a nice chat'. However, digital media are less transparent in vocal work. The limitations of Zoom are reflected in the felt loss of not singing together, which disrupts the collective sense of togetherness. While embracing a new model of practice, many participants are clear that online delivery is a 'make-do' or 'good enough for now' measure before returning to 'the real thing'. But for all the transformations, both desirable and reductive, the experience has been largely positive. Participants marvel at being able to collaborate with those who are overseas and are grateful for the opportunity to continue their creative engagement during the COVID-19 pandemic. These groups are not simply biding time but are embracing the challenge to bring creativity into their homes.

National lockdowns, physical distancing requirements, and shielding of vulnerable groups during the pandemic led to the adoption of video conferencing tools for remote delivery at an unprecedented pace. Platforms such as Zoom enable performing arts practice to continue in challenging circumstances. No longer confined to particular physical settings, music and dance activities can extend into private homes. This has potential for widening participation, reaching individuals for whom mobility is difficult and those living in remote locations. Nevertheless, online delivery, as one participant comments, 'in some ways [...] narrows participation to people who've got the technology and the willingness to learn'. Digital exclusion or inequality and resistance to online delivery are both factors that warrant further research and consideration because there is great potential for online community arts provision.

References

Adams, C. and Thompson, T. L. (2011). Interviewing Objects: Including Educational Technologies as Qualitative Research Participants. *International Journal of Qualitative Studies in Education*, 24(6), pp. 733–750.

Adams, C. and Thompson, T. L. (2016). *Researching a Posthuman World: Interviews with Digital Objects*. London: Palgrave Macmillan.

Friedberg, A. (2006). *The Virtual Window: From Alberti to Microsoft*. Boston: MIT Press

Ihde, D. (1990). *Technology and the Lifeworld: From Garden to Earth*. Indiana: Indiana University Press.

Ihde, D. (2002). *Bodies in Technology*. Minnesota: University of Minnesota Press.

Ihde, D. (2015). Preface. In: R. Rosenberger and P. P. Verbeek, eds., *Postphenomenological Investigations: Essays on Human-Technology Relations*. Maryland: Lexington Books. pp. vii–xvi.

Moustakas, C. (1994). *Phenomenological Research Methods*. California: Sage Publications.

O'Neal Irwin, S. (2016). *Digital Media: Human Technology Connection*. Maryland: Lexington Books.

Rosenberger, R. and Verbeek, P. P. (2015). A Field Guide to Postphenomenology. In: R. Rosenberger and P. P. Verbeek, eds., *Postphenomenological Investigations: Essays on Human-Technology Relations*. Maryland: Lexington Books. pp. 9–42.

10 *not panicky*

Rachel Clive in collaboration with Hughie McIntyre, Euan Hayton, Chloe Maxwell, and Alison Mackenzie

Rachel Clive is a freelance theatre practitioner, interdisciplinary researcher and writer whose research interests include dialogical theatre, performances of human/nonhuman entanglement and neurodiversity. Euan Hayton, Chloe Maxwell, Alison Mackenzie, and Hughie McIntyre are performers whose specific interests include environmental and autistic activism, dance, photography/film and histories of learning disability respectively.

not panicky is a neurodivergent-led dialogical performance piece that was created by performers Euan Hayton, Chloe Maxwell, Alison Mackenzie, and Hughie McIntyre, in collaboration with theatre practice-based researcher Rachel Clive at the University of Glasgow. It was the final piece in a series of five participatory performance-as-research projects with rivers which are called collectively *The Panarchy Projects*. *not panicky* was a response to the heightened anxieties around human/nonhuman 'entanglement' and 'contamination' (Tsing, 2015) that were prevalent in the first phase of the COVID-19 pandemic. It was made in relationship with the tidal part of the River Clyde network, and it explored how connecting performatively with rivers might alleviate human distress and nurture practices of solidarity in a time of environmental crisis. The piece was created largely outdoors in the greater Glasgow area and was first shared with three physically distanced live audiences of 15 members each, in the James Arnott Theatre in Glasgow. This live performance run took place in September 2020, between the first and second UK lockdowns. During the second and third lockdowns, *not panicky* was adapted to a digital format and shared in a series of intimate dialogical performance events on Zoom.

The *not panicky* ensemble formed in Spring 2020 from a larger collective of 12 neurodivergent (mostly learning-disabled and autistic) performers based across Central Scotland. This larger collective had

DOI: 10.4324/9781003165644-14

been meeting at the University of Glasgow prior to the first COVID-19 lockdown in order to create a piece of theatre in connection with the Rivers Forth and Clyde. When this project had to be abandoned due to the pandemic, some performers wanted to stay in touch and continue working with one another. After securing ethical clearance from the University, the project moved online. It soon became clear that not everyone had equal access to the Internet and digital technology. In addition, several people had no desire to meet digitally. Although we were careful to support and accommodate each other's different communication needs and preferences, we found that some of the digital inequalities we were facing were structural, and beyond the scope and resources of the performance project to resolve. As restrictions eased in the Summer of 2020, some of the performers in the River Clyde catchment, who lived fairly close to each other, began meeting up physically, witnessing each other's connections with the parks and the rivers closest to their homes, and sharing stories and survival strategies. At first, only two or three people could meet at once – masked and physically distanced from one another – but gradually, as guidelines allowed, this number increased to five. It was this group of five that became the *not panicky* ensemble. We agreed as a collective to retain a performance focus on our diverse connections with rivers and water, in particular our connections with the River Clyde and its tributaries.

This connection manifested very differently for the four performers. For performer and learning disability activist Hughie McIntyre, the restrictions of the lockdown had awakened traumatic memories of being 'trapped' for 16 years in a residential institution for learning-disabled people in the Campsie hills outside Glasgow. These memories were causing Hughie some anxiety, but focussing on his connection with the River Clyde reminded him of a 'magical' waterfall that had given him strength and solace during that period of his life. Hughie invited the *not panicky* ensemble to visit this waterfall with him, and he created a story of release and liberation, in which he followed the waterfall down the hills to where it meets the River Kelvin, down the Kelvin to the Clyde, from the Clyde to the sea, and back up the Clyde (with the tide) to the city of Glasgow, where he lives now. Following (and flowing with) the rivers alleviated Hughie's anxieties, reminding him that he had survived enforced 'lockdown' before, when he was a much younger man, and would survive it again. Dancer Chloe Maxwell was similarly feeling trapped by the pandemic, and she was interested in exploring the way that 'water moves through the city [...] through buildings and down walls' (*not panicky,* 2020). For Chloe, as for hydrofeminists such as Astrida Neimanis (2017), water is not separate from us but a part of us; it ‘moves through us’, and it ‘needs to be free’ (*not panicky,* 2020) just as we do. Chloe explored this concept through improvised choreographies in her local park, and in the streets around her home in North-East Glasgow. Her work explored the balances, skills, pleasures and freedoms to be found in performing with the local and the everyday. Gymnast and performer Alison Mackenzie was missing physical touch and chose to explore the physical and sensual aspects of her connection with the river she lives by. Alison developed a physical storytelling practice with actual river water and stones, in which she was able to communicate the *pleasure* and *necessity* of reciprocal care and interdependence across human and nonhuman dimensions, something that seemed to resonate particularly strongly with audiences. Environmental activist and performer Euan Hayton wanted to find ways of adapting to change and managing anxiety not solely with regard to the pandemic, and his own autism, but also in relation to the broader issue of climate change (Ray, 2020). Euan felt that the pandemic was a *symptom* of climate change, rather than being separate from it, and his strategies for dealing with the anxieties this insight induced included experimenting with somatic practices and poetry and expressing the love he feels for the natural world. Euan developed a guided relaxation of calm and flow in connection with rivers, which he used first with his co-performers and later with audiences. Euan also wanted to raise awareness about climate change and to engage others in dialogue about adaptation and sustainability.

In the Autumn of 2020, the ensemble was briefly able to rehearse in the James Arnott Theatre at the University of Glasgow, strictly adhering to Scottish Government regulations and University safety guidelines. With support from lighting designer Tony Sweeten, videographer Jassy Earl and dramaturg Susan Worsfold, the ensemble created and staged *not panicky* as a dialogical performance event. The event was structured in three parts. First, performers helped audience members to relax through a gentle relaxation, warm-up and guided visualisation, inviting them to become aware of their own bodyminds and access their own river connections. Second, performers shared insights, questions, and stories from their different explorations with the River Clyde and its tributaries, through a series of interconnected and inter-medial autobiographical performances. Working with video from site-based improvisations, audio from rehearsal processes, fresh river-water and found river materials, the performers brought the river, and their diverse connections with it, into the theatre. Finally, performers invited audiences to discuss the questions they had articulated and explored in their autobiographical performances:

> *How do you adapt to change? What are the biggest issues facing rivers right now? (Euan)*
>
> *What is freedom and movement for you? What does your heart mean to you? (Chloe)*
>
> *What is home for you? What is water for you? (Alison)*
>
> *What does the river mean to you? If you were a sea creature, what would you be? (Hughie)*

Perhaps because they had emerged from performing in connection with rivers in the restricted context of a global pandemic, a context which was affecting everyone present in similar ways, these questions seemed particularly relevant to audiences. Each live performance had a mixed disabled/non-disabled invited audience, all of whom had to provide their personal details for contact tracing purposes and remain physically distanced from one another as well as from the performers throughout the event. The artists were also physically distanced from each other at all times. Despite these restrictive measures, the live piece generated a sense of human intimacy, connection, and communitas. This was in part a result of the performers' collective skills in activating the 'autopoeitic feedback loop' between themselves and the spectators (Fischer-Lichte, 2008), something that created an energy which reminded one attendee of 'the power of being in the room, and sharing space' (personal correspondence). For most live audience members, this was their only visit to the theatre during the first phase of the COVID-19 pandemic. 'It was fantastic to be a part of an audience watching live theatre again', one person told the ensemble afterwards, in response to a request for written feedback. 'I found it very moving and relaxing to be there', another wrote, adding that 'you could feel people relaxing around you as the performance went on'. At least one member of the various audiences found the experience emotionally cathartic. 'Oh, the joy of being in a theatre again!' she wrote, 'I was pulled in immediately, but wasn't prepared to feel so moved. Pulled, because it's my River too'. This audience member had 'tears of connected emotion', as their own 'memories and connections were brought to the surface' (personal correspondence).

Creating a neurodivergent-led performance piece across both digital and physical platforms, in connection with rivers and in the context of a global pandemic led to a number of valuable insights. First, the fact that not everyone could (or had support to) access digital processes and performance events brought attention to the fact that COVID-19 'differentially impacted on disabled people' (Shakespeare et al., 2021: 20). Existing digital and social inequalities were exposed, and new inequalities were created by the pandemic, both of which impacted on the *not panicky* project. Although the project could not resolve these structural inequalities, it could bring attention to them. Second, although performing digitally enabled us to connect with audiences when we had no other options, performing live confirmed that there is no substitute for shared bodily presence in space and time, even if this presence requires us to keep a physical distance from each other. It also revealed that sharing physical space with each other and with audiences can enhance a sense of collective interdependence with regard to our immediate environments, something it proved harder to foster on the digital platform. Third, centring the River Clyde and its tributaries reminded us that even though human/nonhuman entanglement makes us *vulnerable* to contamination, disease, and each other, it is also *essential* to our survival and to our ability to thrive. Performing this entanglement brought attention to our 'response-abilities' (Barad, 2007; Haraway, 2016) across human/nonhuman, as well as across human differences, and inspired feelings of care and pleasure as well as solidarity.

References

Barad, K. (2007). *Meeting the Universe Halfway.* Durham and London: Duke University Press.

Fischer-Lichte, E. (2008). *The Transformative Power of Performance: A New Aesthetics.* London: Routledge.

Haraway, D. (2016). *Staying with the Trouble: Making Kin in the Chthulucene.* Durham: Duke University Press.

Neimanis, A. (2017). *Bodies of Water: Posthumanist Feminist Phenomenology.* London; New York: Bloomsbury Academic.

Ray, S. J. (2020). *A Field Guide to Climate Anxiety: How to Keep your Cool on a Warming Planet.* Oakland: University of California Press.

Shakespeare, T., Watson, N., Brunner, R., Cullingworth, J., Hameed, S., Sherer, N., Pearson, C., and Reichenberger, V. (2021). Disabled People in Britain and the Impact of the COVID-19 Pandemic. *Preprints.* Available at: https://www.preprints.org/manuscript/202101.0563/v1 [accessed 29/01/2021].

Tsing, A. (2015). *The Mushroom at the End of the World: On the Possibility of Life in Capitalist Ruins.* Princeton: Princeton University Press.

11 Invitation

On making together, apart

Gudrun Soley Sigurdardottir

Gudrun Soley Sigurdardottir is an Icelandic performance maker, director, and teaching artist based in Glasgow, Scotland. She works within performance, film, and sound and has a particular interest in the social value of art; delivering work that engages and benefits communities across Scotland and internationally.

This is an invitation;

to reflect
to discover
to reimagine

To consider what *was* and what *is* and the gap between the two;
its limitations and possibilities;
the invitation.

Polmont is Scotland's national holding facility for male young offenders aged between 16 and 21 and is managed by the Scottish Prison Service, an Executive Agency of the Scottish Government. In January 2019, Glass Performance launched Polmont Youth Theatre, based within the Performing Arts Centre at HMYOI Polmont Young Offenders Institution. It is the first youth theatre based in a prison in Scotland and is delivered through a partnership between Glass Performance, Barnardo's and The Scottish Prison Service. Polmont Youth Theatre is a legacy of the Year of Young People (YOYP), 2018, which saw Polmont included in the National Theatre of Scotland's YOYP Futureproof Festival. Members of Polmont Youth Theatre work together as an ensemble to create original devised performance work for audiences of families, their peers, and the wider Arts and Justice community. Glass began working with Barnardo's and Scottish Prison Service in 2017 and has developed a successful partnership over this time. Working in collaboration is a key part of the successful delivery of the projects in Polmont.

DOI: 10.4324/9781003165644-15

Polmont Youth Theatre has always been about coming together to make devised theatre. A space for sharing ideas, opinions and conversations. A space where we create a sense of community. A space.

It has been 52 weeks since we last saw each other. A group of 15 young men in a space with two theatre practitioners, an officer and a youth worker. We sat in a circle, we played games and created movement in pairs. We wrote texts about time and how it shifts depending on the context, which now feels so curiously prescient of what was to come. We had a brief conversation about what was happening in the world, but for most part, we did what we always do. We shook hands at the beginning and the end of the session – a simple, but significant action. A way of marking the beginning and the end; a moment of connection, a warm welcome, an acknowledgement of everyone's presence. And now, a memory and a longing for what *was*.

A gap;

in between myself and the other practitioners, participants, and partners
in knowledge and understanding of how best to respond
in time

There was a moment of confusion, doubt and uncertainty and then a realisation; the engagement had to carry on, somehow. We had to continue our conversations, text-writing and moment-making but, most importantly, to keep connecting with each other. The transition from face-to-face delivery to remote delivery was not straightforward and relied on partnerships and problem-solving, reimagination and collective trust. We had to think quickly; what is the invitation?

> 'A real conversation always contains an invitation. You are inviting another person to reveal herself or himself to you, to tell you who they are or what they want.'
>
> (Whyte, n.d.)

A Way of Passing Time was a 12-week project that engaged young men in a devising process conducted through letter-writing. A written invitation to respond, to write back, to start a dialogue. A space for reflection, personal offerings and creative responses. The letters became a metaphor for a handshake – a moment of connection, a warm welcome, an acknowledgement of everyone's presence. What had started off as a physical exploration of time had become more heightened as we navigated this new way of connecting with each other and passing time together. *A Way of Passing Time* was a response to the unforeseen; an invitation to reimagine participation and introduce possibilities for new collaborations with partners and participants. It showed that connection, community and a creative process can be forged through letter writing.

Engagement is a form of conversation; a bonding experience that requires others and in order to engage others, an invitation is needed. No-one knew how long the first lockdown would last, which meant that the invitation for the participants was open-ended, rather than fixed. This allowed for engagement on multiple levels instead of an invitation either accepted or declined. The participants were not simply joining a process; they were co-creating it alongside the creative team. The project reached young people who previously encountered challenges to participation in a physical space, allowing for a wider engagement and further inclusion; allowing for a wider reach than previous in-person processes. This became a real highlight of the project and sparked new conversations around the increased access and possibilities of one-to-one engagement.

In Tune was a weekly interactive radio show created by and for the young people in Polmont. The project carried on the legacy of *A Way of Passing Time,* where the young people involved engaged in letter-writing to create content and creatively respond to the radio show. The project allowed us to reach the whole prison population, encouraged engagement on multiple levels and allowed for short- and long-term participation. It inspired further collaboration between partners, where the involvement of youth workers and officers became integral to the creative process. *In Tune* allowed us to break down obstacles to participation by directly engaging with the young men in personalised one-to-one conversation, rather than in a seemingly high stakes in-person collaborative setting. The project enabled us to engage not only those who joined the project but those listening too. An invitation to share stories and select a song as a dedication, a song for our hometown, a song that tells a story, that lifts our spirits and takes us back in time. In the second lockdown, the project continued and evolved, where the young men renamed it, *The JukeBox,* and continued to creatively engage with and shape the show. This engagement culminated in three Christmas Special episodes, aired over the festive season, and curated, created, and recorded by a group of ten young men in Polmont. This interactive radio show has become so popular that it is now its own project and accompanies Polmont Youth Theatre.

A formal invitation holds lots of detailed information on when, where, who, what and why. Throughout the pandemic, the answers to these questions were ever-changing and endlessly inconsistent. This open-ended invitation feels like an extension of a handshake – a connection, a warm welcome, an acknowledgement of everyone's presence. The first lockdown forced many of us to pause and to take stock, to re-evaluate what is important and how we spend our time. The reimagining of Polmont Youth Theatre throughout lockdown has reminded me of the importance of being a responsive practitioner, continuously rediscovering and refining what it is that I do. At the heart of it is invitation; creative dialogue that aims for connection with participants, audiences, people. A conversation that allows me to connect with others and the world around me. This is what poet David Whyte refers to as 'the conversational nature of reality' (2011):

> 'Just beyond yourself. It's where you need to be. Half a step into self-forgetting and the rest restored by what you'll meet.'
>
> (Whyte, 2018)

My intention is continuously shifting, rooted in what it was and has been whilst edging towards something else, something yet to be discovered. I am looking for and accepting new invitations that open up possibilities for new connections and an expansion of my practice. I invite you to join me in this act;

to reflect
to discover
to reimagine

To consider what *was* and what *is* and the gap between the two;
its limitations and possibilities;
the invitation.

Polmont Youth Theatre is run by Lead Artist Gudrun Soley Sigurdardottir, Project Manager Louise Allan and Assistants Ricky Williamson and Jack Tully.

Glass Performance is an international award-winning theatre company that gives voice to unheard stories, told by everyday people. Since its inception in 2008, Glass have made performances and co-produced projects on small and large scales – from theatres to nightclubs and football pitches – for an audience of 600 to an audience of just one. Glass works across Scotland but mostly between Glasgow, Dundee and Polmont. All the projects involve real families, communities or individuals and explore their relationships, memories and histories in order to help us all better understand the world we live in together.

Barnardo's deliver the Outside In Youth Work service that supports the development of young people in custody within Polmont; aiming to enhance the skills and build confidence to prepare the young people for successful re-integration into their home communities. Working in partnership with Barnardo's is crucial to the success of Polmont Youth Theatre and ensures a prison wide approach to development and delivery.

References

Whyte, D. (2011). Life at the Frontier: The Conversational Nature of Reality. *TEDxPugetSound.* Available at: https://www.youtube.com/watch?v=5Ss1H-uA1hIk&ab_channel=TEDxTalks [accessed 15/04/2021].

Whyte, D. (2018). *The Bell and the Blackbird.* Langley: Many Rivers Press.

Whyte, D. (n.d.) 10 Questions That Have No Right to Go Away. Available at: *https://static1.squarespace.com/static/56d77489cf80a15f84d55c30/t/578805b96b8f5b162da556c5/1468532153946/David+Whyte+-+10+Questions+That+Have+No+Right+to+Go+Away.pdf* [accessed: 01/02/2021]

IV

Curation

Performing the archive

12 Presence at a distance – Alastair MacLennan and performing drawing in lockdown

Judit Bodor

Dr Judit Bodor is Baxter Fellow in Curatorial Practice (Teaching & Research) at Duncan of Jordanstone College of Art & Design, University of Dundee. Her research is situated at the intersection of 'the curatorial' as a performative mode of knowledge production and the histories and practices of time-based art.

Introduction

How can the liveness of performance be sustained through mediated presence? How can performance artists reach audiences at times of physical isolation? What are the inherent difficulties and opportunities within performance art that curators can draw upon to respond to these questions after the COVID-19 pandemic? In this chapter, I discuss how Adam Lockhart and I exhibited Alastair MacLennan's body of performance drawing, *LIM(I)NAL,* produced during the lockdown, using the artist's new archive website (amaclennan-archive.ac.uk) hosted by the University of Dundee as our curatorial platform. To do so, I first outline and contextualise MacLennan's work and practice identifying its key features and parameters upon which we developed our curatorial approach. I then briefly situate the artist's concept of 'actuation' within the broader field of performance art to consider how liveness is mediated and made manifest in these works before describing how MacLennan shifted his practice toward an interrelated approach to performance drawing and performance for camera under lockdown conditions. I discuss examples of how the resulting video work, *VIAL AVAIL (presence of absence)*, has been curated online and offline internationally between May and September 2020 before outlining our approach to the *LIM(I)NAL* exhibition and its accompanying Zoom-event *IN AND EASE* over November-December 2020. I conclude by considering the extent to which potentially literal and

DOI: 10.4324/9781003165644-17

inflexible notions of liveness applied to performance art disguise a fluidity and serendipity at the heart of MacLennan's practice which enforces, not distracts, from the holistic core and outlook of his work.

Alastair MacLennan and art as 'actuation'

Alastair MacLennan is internationally recognised for what he terms 'actuations': tableau-like visual art performances occurring over extended continuous durations of hours or even days in a broad range of artistic and everyday environments. To date, he has presented over 600 of these works in performance art festivals and exhibitions across Asia, Europe and America and represented Ireland at the Venice Biennale in 2014. In addition to his solo practice, his work has also influenced the development of performance collaborations exploring duration, context and simultaneity, such as with Black Market International (since 1989), Belfast-based collective beyond (since 2001), and in a long-standing collaboration with artist Sandra Johnston (since 2009). Most of these actuations have been meticulously documented on slide film, providing the basis of significant retrospective exhibitions and catalogues (*Alastair MacLennan Is No 1975–1988*, 1988; and *Alastair MacLennan Knot Naught*, 2003) and his comprehensive archive hosted physically and online by the artist's 1960s alma mater, Duncan of Jordanstone College of Art & Design, University of Dundee.

MacLennan's actuations are characterised by the durational unfolding of images and actions 'in-situ' in response to various sites and contexts, most often through the co-presence of live encounter at the heart of the aesthetic experience. He derives the term from conceptually combining the verb 'to actuate', meaning 'to cause to do', with the adjective 'actual', meaning 'existing in fact; as real' (… as distinct from the ideal' […]. Emphasis is on what is real in the present moment' (MacLennan, n.d.). Conceived according to the Buddhist principles he has studied since the 1970s, MacLennan's actuations reject binary thinking to seek the 'interfusion' of art and life, privilege being present in the actual moment, and engage with the world through 'real' rather than metaphoric actions. MacLennan describes 'being present' as coming to terms with 'aspects of living which are raw and problematic, but also convey means to overcome escapist attitudes and negative forces we allow to infiltrate our lives' (Stewart, 1983). Further elaborated in Bakhtinian terms by Roddy Hunter (2003: 184), MacLennan's actuations ask us to be 'answerable' in our thoughts and deeds in the respective worlds of culture and life 'to realise that each of us can have "no alibi"'. In these terms, the work foregrounds moral and ethical accountability between artist, their work, audience and world.

Unsurprisingly, actuations are grounded by a shared situational experience in which liveness is of pivotal importance. Presence becomes 'co-presence' during the real-time unfolding of an actuation. Multiple subject-object relations between artist, audience, objects and site emerge and, at times, synthesise to become an indivisible and non-hierarchical entity. In this context, objects and subjects perform affectively through proximity and interconnection, and thus the artwork becomes a flat ontology. Boris Nieslony (quoted in *Alastair MacLennan Knot Knaught*, 2003: 49), performance artist and long-term collaborator as member of Black Market International, described experiencing a MacLennan actuation as an 'indefinable feeling' and being captured by the 'energy' and the 'charged emotion' of the space. The auratic aesthetic of MacLennan's work aligns with Black Market's operating principle as an 'open system of BEGEGNUNG (encountering) without fixed spaces or fixed themes' (Nieslony, 1999). The artist's actuations contributed over the years to the international collective's idiomatic form of performance where several artists meet to perform alone and together simultaneously, in parallel, as a microcosm of interconnection, similarly to other contemporary groups such as Bbeyond, with whom MacLennan also works to this day.

Curating performance then and now, here and there

A key challenge for curating performance art from its archives is how to overcome the historical gap between an event and its reception in a later exhibition. Far from being a flat ontology, archival exhibition contexts often refer to the live, in-person experience of the historical performance as being of primary value and later engagement with the work through forms of, usually photographic, documentation as somewhat insufficient and secondary. The inflexible view of an ontological opposition between live and mediatised performance, and between primary event and secondary documentation – associated most notably with Peggy Phelan (1993) – has been discussed and critiqued across performance studies, art history and curating since the 1990s. Philip Auslander argues that sometimes the 'space of the document [...] becomes the only place in which the performance occurs' (Auslander, 2006: 2), citing Yves Klein's *Leap into the Void* (1960), which captures Klein in flight, having launching himself from a building seemingly without falling back to earth. He adds that the act of documentation itself can also performatively frame 'actions as performance' (Auslander, 2014: n.pg.), citing Vito Acconci's *Trademarks* (1970). This work comprises photography of Acconci biting his body and handwritten and typed text of the experience, thus exploring different ways in which an action can leave its trace.

The vexed relationship between performance and its documentation and archives has also become a generative site of discourse and practice from a curatorial perspective, particularly in the last ten years. The boundaries of what constitutes performance have been interrogated and expanded through cross-disciplinary close readings and notions such as 'viral' ontology (Bedford, 2012), 'changeability' (Hölling, 2016) and 'variability' (Rinehart and Ippolito, 2014) and the rethinking of the archive from 'repository' to 'repertoire' (Taylor, 2003). Regardless of the theoretical discourse – and as I have discussed elsewhere (Bodor, 2019) – the problem remains that whether we work with interpretive, documentary, or performative documents, curating historical performance can quickly turn the shared live experience of events into the detached experience of static portable objects in later exhibition contexts. The question then is how to construct an aesthetic experience where the document and the event can be considered as materially different actualisations of performance. Enforcement of travel restrictions and physical distancing during COVID-19 intensified the issue of 'liveness' and added a geographical dimension to our existing question of how to create a 'living archive' of performative engagement with the body, context and legacy of MacLennan's works.

Recording, scoring, corresponding: making *VIAL AVAIL (presence of absence)*

Curators of performance art worldwide needed to rethink their approach to previously planned events and festivals in light of the unfolding pandemic from early 2020. Adaptation to online, offline or hybrid formats of display seemed the immediate alternative to cancellation. Working curatorially through these formats resulted in the exploration of synchronous and asynchronous liveness experienced by audiences, one way or another, at a physical distance. MacLennan, unable to travel and confined to the surroundings of his home and studio, similarly needed to rethink his approach to making performance for these adjusted curatorial contexts. One dilemma was whether, for example, to present work live and online or as pre-recorded performance for camera. The former privileges liveness through co-presence in time, while the latter sacrifices in-person proximity to retain sufficient influence over the work's framing and composition. One of the attractions of performance-for-camera is that it enables the performance image as a portable object designed rather than undermined by its status as a portable object.

MacLennan's preference for the 'real' over the artificial does not preclude his existing daily practice of performance drawing and even performance for camera, which became increasingly foregrounded during the COVID-19 pandemic. Translating his practice to video in particular, however, has not been straightforward. While the artist is not against documentation, as seen from the thousands of slides in his archive, he has not favoured moving image formats such as film or video in the past. Notwithstanding his interest in exploring performance for video in *Alchemist* (2010), produced with film-maker Richard Ashrowan and artist Sandra Johnston, MacLennan usually prefers photography to video when it comes to documenting his own works, as the moving image lens does not tolerate the slow, durational unfolding of imagery.

> For much of the documentation of past performances I preferred still photos and slides, as many of those performances involved actual, or inferred 'stillness'… and where 'movement' was engaged in some performances, it was meditative and mindful… and I found the (sometimes) unreflective, sloppy, jerky, handling of movement of the video camera, by some documenters, at odds with how / what I wished the work to convey. I'd be very happy for my performances to be filmed, in an appropriately attuned, sensitive way.
>
> (A MacLennan, personal correspondence, April 12, 2021)

Given these concerns regarding the 'unreflective' nature of the recorded moving image, it might seem surprising that during the COVID-19 pandemic the artist accepted invitations to submit performance on video for performance art festivals in Poland, England, China, and Hong Kong. However, as I argue here, MacLennan's approach to performance-for-camera is not a video documentation of performance intended primarily for in-person proximity but an artwork in its own right. The work engages audiences directly but differently from his in-person performances and draws on the artist's ability to make performance in response to a new online context.

MacLennan's 'lockdown' performance-for-camera *VIAL AVAIL (presence of absence),* comprises four versions (a, b, c, d) of a 7:36 minute-long edited footage of one performance shot in the artist's garden in Greenisland, Belfast on May 2, 2020. The versions were edited with photographer Jordan Hutchings' assistance who has documented the artist's work for many years. In version 'a' of the video, MacLennan sits at the skeletal metal entrance of what might once have been a greenhouse. His figure is framed centrally and clothed in black. He wears a white respiratory mask and a broken pair of sunglasses with white and red tape hanging from his neck to his feet – all but the mask are signature MacLennan imagery. To his left and behind semi-transparent glass are his drawings. In front of him is a bucket. He picks up his drawings one-by-one, presents them to the camera, and sets them on fire with a lighter before dropping them into the bucket. In version 'b', the video footage moves backwards, so it looks like the artist is 'unburning' the drawings. Versions 'c' and 'd' also play the video sequence forward and backwards, burning and unburning the drawings, but this time the image is cropped, revealing only the artist's hands and the drawings in close-up. As in many previous performances – the artist's own word to refer to works 'in person' – the soundtrack is a list of spoken words, this time using verbs from daily newspapers selected as 'the result of blinkered thinking and "selected facts" in what constitutes "news"' (MacLennan, 2020). The soundtrack is the same (never reversed) across all four versions of the video, thus it does not follow the same logic as the visual image sequence.

VIAL AVAIL (presence of absence) emerged from MacLennan's daily drawing practice, the performative aspects of which have become more pronounced during COVID-19. From March 2020 onwards, he made hundreds of drawings on paper, each signed on the back with the title *LIM(I)NAL*, emphasising that they are considered as both a singular 'entity' and 'as part of a continuous "flow"' within a long durational and indefinite performative artwork. As MacLennan explained (personal correspondence, March 1, 2021) 'all my future drawings/works on paper will continue to be titled *LIM(I)NAL*, until the COVID-19 virus lockdown is over'. To make the drawings the artist uses a method where he draws with both hands simultaneously using his peripheral vision while focusing on a soaked and scrunched up paper tissue placed between two A2 size sheets of paper. Regarding the 'blank page as a metaphor of infinity, out of which everything manifests, and into which all recedes, endlessly' he draws with materials that 'normally' don't mix, like oil, charcoal and ink, to experiment with their material 'interbeing' (A MacLennan, personal communication, 6 October 2020). Each piece is laid out on the studio floor for days to dry while he continues to produce more drawings. Once dried, he balances the composition of drawings he likes with added texts, marks made with rubber and other materials, while Jordan Hutchings continuously documents both his action and its outcomes as digital photographic images. The drawings seen being burnt in the videos were those that MacLennan was not satisfied with, others were selected for a special edition titled *A WAIVE*, which the artist sent in groups of 20 to the curators of his *VIAL AVAIL* video suggesting the possibility of a physical exhibition. The remainder of drawings, both as physic artworks and digitally photographed, are retained for later addition to his archive in Dundee.

VIAL AVAIL (presence of absence) in online, offline and hybrid curatorial formats

MacLennan has sent different versions of his *VIAL AVAL* video with editions of his *A WAIVE* drawings in response to invitations to participate in events and exhibitions during the COVID-19 pandemic. In Poland, the 2020 edition of *CONTEXTS Festival of Ephemeral Art* (Sokołowsko, 23–26 July), curated by Marta Czyż and Malgorzata Sady, became a hybrid online/offline festival. The 'local choreographies' section consisted of performances for audiences on site, which were then streamed online to engage with a potentially global audience. In contrast, the online programme of 'loneliness' comprised of pre-recorded works (documentation of performance or performance-for-camera), which were projected in a cinema for local audiences during the festival and later also streamed on the festival's website (konteksty.live). Due to a delay in delivery, MacLennan's physical drawings did not arrive in time to be exhibited, and were replaced by the streaming of a four -minute slideshow of digital photographs as part of the festival preview programme on the 23 July, followed by version 'a' of *VIAL AVAIL* on the 26 July. Version 'b' of the video launched the *]ps[screens* programme of the Folkstone-based artist-led group]performance s p a c e[on 1 June and was also accessible for local audiences as a window-display alongside Alicia Radage's video piece *17* (2020). Version 'c' was shown on a flat screen monitor as part of MacLennan's physical solo exhibition at the *8th GUYU Action Contemporary Performance Art Festival* between 10 and 23 September. As seen on the photographic documentation on GUYU ACTION Facebook page (10 September 2020), the exhibition also included 20 of MacLennan's *A WAIVE* drawings. Finally, version 'd' was streamed by The Originals, an artists' group in Hong Kong, hosted on their Facebook page on 8 May. While all four contexts experimented with online dissemination of performance, only the version streamed on Facebook from Hong Kong archived the work for future audiences.

Curating *LIM(I)NAL* and *IN AND EASE*

Like all these other curators, Adam Lockhart and I had to devise a curatorial strategy to present MacLennan's performance works during the pandemic. Instead of showing the pre-recorded *VIAL AVAIL* video, we conceived an online performative exhibition of the source work, MacLennan's drawing-as-performance called *LIM(I)NAL*, accompanied by a Zoom-performance event, *IN AND EASE.* This was the first curatorial project on the artist's website since the acquisition of MacLennan's physical archive by Duncan of Jordanstone College of Art & Design in 2019. Our strategy combined Lockhart's ongoing digitisation project of the archival material with a new multi-modal research project, *What is a Living Archive? Curating the Unruly Archives of Contemporary Art?* that I initiated to explore new approaches to curatorial research and interaction with time-based art archives held in Dundee. The online exhibition idea emerged from our conversations with the artist about how to make his drawing-as-performance work publicly available as a living art archive.

The exhibition presented digital photographic documentation of the artist's works side by side with drawings by others received through an open call-in response to the artist's score, as follows:

1 Choose one of the following scores:

   A Draw your breathing process
   B Do a drawing in which 'looking' transitions to 'seeing'.
   C Draw your sense of actual (not conceptual) 'interfusion' between the primary elements (earth, water, fire, air)

2 Make a portrait format drawing on paper with your chosen implement(s)

These instructions were also exhibited to provide insight into the artist's working process and encourage an understanding of the performative dimensions of mark-making, of drawing-as-performance. The growing sequence of drawings displayed on the website as a continuous loop expressed a state of 'becoming' exhibited and archived at once. The exhibition evolved 'live' over two months during November-December 2020 and is now accessible as 'archived' on the project website. *IN AND EASE* (26 November 2020), as titled by MacLennan, was an online colloquium with practitioners exploring the subject of MacLennan's approach to drawing-as-performance. The event's centrepiece was a live, synchronous drawing workshop led by MacLennan which enabled participants to work/perform alone but in the presence of others at a time of physical isolation, on the 'drawing breath' score and produce drawings for the online exhibition, *LIM(I)NAL*. The workshop was bracketed by contributions from artists Roddy Hunter, Tania Kovats and Sandra Johnston, whose respective practices intersect with MacLennan's work in different ways.

Roddy Hunter created a video work, *Drawing Remains, Drawings Remain*, which comprised a performed reading of a text he wrote for MacLennan's exhibition catalogue *LIE TO LAY* (Hunter, 2017). The video work drew performatively on writing as a textual and visual editing process to align particular images of MacLennan's drawings between 1976 and 2020 with a spoken word soundtrack. It offered a reading of the symbiotic 'both/and' relationship between performance and drawing as 'two sides of the same coin as action and reflection' and of 'the images imagined to become actions, to be later embodied, to score and be scored as an inscription on the surface' (Hunter, 2017: 41). The video – now accessible on the Alastair MacLennan Archive website – expands on the earlier written piece by rendering its visual poetry on the page performative through moving image and speech.

Sandra Johnston responded to the 'drawing breath' score with two new drawings that she introduced and discussed in the event in relation to her experience of live performance collaborations with MacLennan. She described her relationship to drawing breath as an uneasy process of becoming attuned to the inner energy of the body. She shared images of her drawings made over two-hour periods, working simultaneously with both hands and with her eyes closed while moving around a table. She described the bodily experience of breathing while making these drawings, describing it as allowing 'the hands to do a complicated dance on the page' to chart the sensation that defines the drawing outside on paper. Johnson's approach to drawing was built on her memory of years of collaboration with MacLennan. She compared the process of finding a rhythm in drawing breathing to finding moments of 'equilibrium' and 'attunement' in the lived experience of drawing together with MacLennan over a six-day durational performance, *Aligning 2,* at Customs House Gallery in South Shields (2015). As she concluded, the moment of equilibrium in both drawing and live performance is 'the perfect point of connection' where materials, bodies and actions – often with different characteristics – 'interfuse'.

The third artist, Tania Kovats, had no previous knowledge of MacLennan's drawing as performance work, but her longstanding practice combining meditation with exploratory drawing aligns with MacLennan's interests. The colloquium presented an opportunity for the two artists to meet and draw together, so to speak, in dialogue. In her presentation, Kovats distinguished between drawing as a process of material exploration and drawing as creating representations of a preconceived mental image or space. She revealed her performative approach to making drawing work by describing her experiences of drawing water and drawing breath, uncannily recalling Johnston's earlier discussion. She shared a process of flooding paper with ink and seawater, then letting the drawing emerge as salt crystallises on the surface – in this respect, she shares an interest with MacLennan in enabling material agency to determine the work, while questioning the importance of the artist's intentionality. In her response to MacLennan's score, Kovats' material sensibility extended to drawing *with* the body. She made her drawings in response to MacLennan's score through 'emptying her lungs on the paper', breathing into a small puddle of ink which rises into a bubble filled with exhalation and allowing it to burst.

Conclusion: liveness, digitisation, and distance

It is clear that MacLennan has sustained different forms of 'liveness' as a mediated presence in the context of online and hybrid exhibitions during the COVID-19 pandemic. In deciding to send different versions of his performance-for-camera work to various festivals, MacLennan made a judgment that distance in time and space, in other words, being 'less live' does not undermine the quality of the work's aesthetic encounter. In the four video versions of *VIAL AVAIL (presence of absence)* the artist used editing as a cinematic tool to control the aesthetic experience aligned with the principle of 'interfusion' (both/and) that is at the heart of every actuation. He not only included zooming in and out to allow both full-frame and close-up view, but also created a reverse imagery of burning and 'unburning' of drawings, an action which could not have been experienced in a live performance. The four videos exemplify Philip Auslander's argument (2014) regarding the 'performativity of performance documentation' where the document constitutes, rather than illustrates, a performance. Furthermore, by sending different versions of the video to varying festivals under the same title, MacLennan's work has unfolded over the year. As a body of work, the four videos will be brought together and made publicly accessible at once for the first time on the artist's website to coincide with this chapter's publication.

In analysing the curatorial contexts of MacLennan's works during COVID-19, we might also ask how curatorial practice around performance art has adjusted to performance at a distance. In most cases of exhibiting MacLennan's works, the curators' approach remained 'analogue', using online platforms to show pre-recorded documentation or examples of performance-for-camera. From this perspective, *IN AND EASE* and *LIM(I)NAL* were distinct, as they engaged with the archiving, afterlives, and future engagement with the work as part of the online display. The digital exhibition and colloquium at once presented and archived the performance, thus opening up a way to develop MacLennan's archive as an active, performative curatorial project. Curating living archives was initially concerned with performatively engaging the historical distance between the work as documentation and the present moment of engagement. MacLennan's work has compounded and compelled this distance by the need for 'co-presence' across geographical and historical sites, which was best achieved through *IN AND EASE*. At the same time, *LIM(I)NAL* launched the archive website as an accumulative depository of digitised documentation and as the basis of a living, breathing archive generating new work and insights.

References

Auslander, P. (2014). 'Surrogate Performances. Performance Documentation and the New York avant-garde, ca. 1964–74.' In: E. Carpenter, ed., *On performativity*, Minneapolis: Walker Art Centre. Available at: http://walkerart.org/collections/publications/performativity/surrogate-performances [accessed 19/04/2021].

Auslander, P. (2006). "The Performativity of Performance Documentation." *PAJ: A Journal of Performance and Art*, 28(3), pp. 1–10.

Bedford, C. (2012). The Viral Ontology of Performance. In: A. Jones and A. Heathfield, eds., *Perform, Repeat, Record. Live Art in History*. London: Intellect. pp. 77–89.

Bodor, J. (2019). The "Extended Life" of Performance. Curating 1960s Multimedia Art in the Contemporary Museum. In: H. B. Hölling, F. G. Bewer and K. Ammann, eds., *The Explicit Material. Inquiries on the Intersection of Curatorial and Conservation Cultures*. Leiden-Boston: Brill. pp. 117–142.

Hölling, H. B. (2016). The Aesthetics of Change. On the Relative Durations of the Impermanent. In: E. Hermens and F. Robertson, eds., *Authenticity in Transition: Changing Practices in Contemporary Art Making and Conservation*. London: Archetype Publications. pp. 13–24.

Hunter, R. (2003). A Place to Place; a Sight to See. In: H. Mulholland, ed., *Alastair MacLennan. Knot Naught*. Belfast: Ormeau Baths Gallery. pp. 177–185.

Hunter, R. (2017). Drawing Remains, Drawings Remain. In: *Alastair MacLennan. Lie to Lay* [exhibition catalogue] Edinburgh: Summerhall. pp. 40–41.

MacLennan, A. (n.d.). *Actuation* [manuscript]. Alastair MacLennan Archive, University of Dundee.

MacLennan, A. (2020). Alastair MacLennan. *Contexts Ephemeral Art Festival website*. Available at: https://konteksty.live/en/alaistair-maclennan/ [accessed 21/02/2021]

Nieslony, B. (1999). The Performances of BLACK MARKET INTERNATIONAL. *Studio Plesungan*. Available at: https://studioplesungan.org/undisclosed-territory/undisclosed-territory-4/black-market-international/ [accessed 19/04/2021].

Phelan, P. (1993). *Unmarked. The Politics of Performance*. London: Routledge.

Rinehart, R. and Ippolito, J. (2014). *Re-collection. Art, New Media, and Social Memory*. Cambridge: The MIT Press.

Snoddy, S. ed. (1988). *Alastair MacLennan. Is No 1975–1988*. Bristol: Arnolfini.

Stewart, N. (1983). Alastair MacLennan interviewed by Nick Stewart. *Circa*, 13. Available at: https://amaclennan-archive.ac.uk/2020/11/18/circa-magazine-no-13/ [accessed 19/04/2021].

Taylor, D. (2003). *The Archive and the Repertoire. Cultural Memory and Performance in the Americas*. Durham: Duke University Press.

13 Recording *My Body, My Archive* at Tate Modern

A collision course of curating on the eve of COVID-19

Tamsin Hong

Tamsin Hong is Assistant Curator at Tate Modern specialising in Performance, curating performances by Nedko Solakov, Franz Erhard Walther, and Boris Charmatz. She has curated *A Year in Art: Australia 1992* at Tate Modern, building on her experience in contemporary Aboriginal and Torres Strait Islander art.

Days before it was due to open at Tate Modern, we were forced to cancel the 2020 BMW Tate Live Exhibition, *Our Bodies Our Archives*, due to the then recently declared COVID-19 pandemic. I was the Assistant Curator working with Catherine Wood, Senior Curator of the Live programme on the exhibition which featured artists Faustin Linyekula, Okwui Okpokwasili, and Tanya Lukin Linklater. Each artist's practice presents the body as a challenge to value systems reflected in Western museums, using their dance-based methodologies to interrupt object-based narratives, particularly those built on colonial legacies. These practices have seemingly become more urgent since George Floyd's death on 25 May 2020, sparking renewed Black Lives Matter protests. The protests combined with reports on the disparate effects of the COVID-19 pandemic on 'BAME' communities in the UK and the ensuing calls to re-evaluate racial equality in the arts all reached critical peaks during the pandemic (Harbison, 2020). Within this context, and given that Linyekula, Okpokwasili, and Lukin Linklater's distinct practices present the resilience of the body in the face of colonisation, the cancellation of the Live Exhibition was even more tragic. Wood and I explained how each artist uses 'the body in different ways to explore history, inheritance and storytelling', raising 'questions about shared memory, visibility and the relationship between material culture and immaterial tradition, challenging what these ideas mean within the context of a modern art museum' (Tate, 2020).

DOI: 10.4324/9781003165644-18

Yet even amidst the increasingly changing environment in the weeks and days leading up to the closure of Tate Modern on 18 March 2020, we had begun to sense the historic moment within which we were operating and therefore the significance of our achievement in recording what we could of the exhibition. While Okpokwasili and Lukin Linklater were unable to travel to London amidst borders closing and flight cancellations, Linyekula and his collaborators – who were already in London – were able to create a one-off performance-to-camera of *My Body, My Archive,* the inspiration behind the exhibition's title. A year later, as I reflect on these events, I share with you the ambition of the never-seen exhibition and its planned performances in the subterranean Tanks at Tate Modern, focusing on the presentation of Linyekula's work. I contextualise these ambitions as they changed shape, illustrating how we rapidly responded to the ever-changing realities of the initial stages of the pandemic. In considering the recording of Linyekula's *My Body, My Archive,* I reflect on how the themes it raises around fragility, social connection and the environment have resonated and amplified during the pandemic.

The ambition

The Live Exhibition was planned for 19–29 March 2020, as the latest iteration of Tate's commissioning Live programme, with a complex offering of performances, durational participatory practices, open rehearsals, installation, video, and an artists' panel discussion. The ambition was to provide a comprehensive programme of Linyekula, Okpokwasili, and Lukin Linklater's work, who were brought together because 'of their distinct practices grown from dance, [where] each artist is concerned with how history is held in the body: how the body itself might represent an archive that is distinct from written history, or images' (Wood and Hong, 2020: 6). Tate Modern visitors would be able to encounter aspects of each artist's work without charge through installations, available during opening hours. There were also free and ticketed performances scheduled throughout the ten days. Okpokwasili was preparing to bring her collaborative practice *Sitting on a Man's Head* during the day and perform *Poor People's TV Room Solo* over three evenings, finishing the exhibition with a procession aimed at bringing strangers together. Beginning with open rehearsals in the daytime, Lukin Linklater was to present *women: iskwewak* in dialogue with her site-specific installation in the South Tank, sharing her practice created from long-term collaborations and interactions with her extended Alutiiq and Cree family. The only performance which was to eventuate was Linyekula's new retrospective work, *My Body, My Archive*. It was to be reflected in smaller, intimate performances as well as an installation of his work which included video, light and sculptural components. Through examining the original intention behind the retrospective of Linyekula's work, I consider his exhibition presentation in terms of two aspects critical to Linyekula's framework: the body as archive, and the significance of the circle as a collaborative concept.

The notion of a retrospective in performance art has often focused on documentation of historic events through video and photographic recordings. In working with Linyekula, the intention was to create a live retrospective, bringing together selections from his autobiographical performances to create *My Body, My Archive*. Each work presents a different facet of Linyekula's reflection of his country, the Democratic Republic of Congo (DRC), and how nation-building is felt in the intimate lives of those experiencing it. The earliest work, *Sur les traces de Dinozord* (In Search of Dinozord, 2012), weaves a story between Linyekula and his companions as they retrace their shared history in Kisangani and recount memories of old friends and the dreams lost while history and conflict collided with their personal journeys. *Statue of Loss* (2014) is Linyekula's monument to First World War Congolese veterans, using official reports, letters, and recordings to commemorate their role in the European-lead war. Taking its name from Linyekula's ancestral village, *Banataba* (2017) is a performance inspired by a statue from Linyekula's matrilineal clan in the Metropolitan Museum of Art's collection. Linyekula states the statue was 'considered of minor importance by the curators and thus kept in storage', setting in motion his return to his mother's village, and resulting in the performance 'to symbolically bring back this statue to the place it belongs to, to people it used to/should talk to (Linyekula and Dupray, 2018)'. In *Congo* (2019), Linyekula creates a choreographic dialogue between contemporary dance and the historic narrative of the colonisers, drawing from Eric Vuillard's book of the same name. In bringing these four performances together, Linyekula creates a live retrospective of his work as a choreographic storyteller through his critique of Western knowledge.

Central to these performances, and reflecting tendencies in his wider practice, is Linyekula's collaborative methodology. He conceptualises his process in terms of a circle: as energy passes from one shoulder to the next, it creates a circle which Linyekula conceives as an energetic support structure. For Linyekula, his sense of self is intrinsically part of the circle, stating that the individual cannot sustain themselves alone, they need a circle of companions to sustain momentum and to support knowledge generation (Linyekula, 2020). This not only incorporates people he collaborates with in a specific moment and place, but also includes companions from different locations and from the past and future. He thereby continually replenishes the circle as an alternative model of ephemerality, which is distinctly not fragile. This evokes Nassim Taleb's concept of 'antifragility' which 'is beyond resilience or robustness, the resilient resists shocks and stays the same; the antifragile gets better' (2012: 17). A crucial site for Linyekula's antifragile circle is his Studios Kabako in the DRC. The studio describes itself as 'people crazy enough to believe stubbornly, despite the upheavals of history, wars, revolutions, regimes, in the celebration of beauty' (Studios Kabako, 2021). Linyekula was particularly excited at the prospect of bringing together his global collaborators to Tate. He had worked with many artists in North America, Europe and Africa, but they had not yet had the opportunity to work with each other. Linyekula was also keen to extend his circle to future collaborators based in London and had begun forging potential connections before his arrival. The envisioned manifestation of this approach was to be small, salon-like jam sessions held within the Transformers (part of the Tanks space) where his installation was displayed. In these sessions he intended to bring together collaborators and specific audiences such as musicians, dancers, and neighbours, thereby expanding the circle.

Complementing Linyekula's performances was an installation incorporating light, sound, video, and sculpture in the Transformers. This included videos reflecting the performances integrated into *My Body, My Archive*. Projected on one wall was footage of Linyekula travelling to Banataba on the Congo River. On the opposite wall was a projection of a ritual from *Statue of Loss* where Linyekula uses white paint to write onto his body the names of people and places which create his identity. Interspersed were quotes and poems used in *My Body, My Archive* which resonated with Linyekula's experience of recent history, such as:

> How will I walk to myself
> To my people
> With my blood on fire
> And my history in ruins?
>
> – Adonis

Linyekula reflected in conversations with Wood and I on the experience of waking up one day and hearing the radio announce that the country he was born in, Zaire, no-longer existed and had become the DRC. Poetry and quotes became a crucial part of Linyekula's expression of this experience, explaining 'it's writing that lead me to performance and the body'. His practice includes examining the limitations of Western-based written history in contrast to knowledge held within the body. Dance, for him, is a way to draw out ancient knowledge that cannot be adequately expressed in words. In bringing this approach to the Live Exhibition, Linyekula uses the metaphor of singular light bulbs flickering in the shadows: their resistance to being swallowed up by the darkness reflects Linyekula's feelings about himself within the history of the DRC. This resistance also reflects the role of his art within the socio-economic and political instability of his country, and as a form of agitation within the knowledge structures and value systems typically represented by the post-enlightenment model of the museum. Linyekula's approach inherently challenges the colonial legacies imbedded within the museum, but these simmering issues came to a head within the context of pandemic and the Black Lives Matter protests in the Summer of 2020 with the pandemic's exposure of local and global divisions demarcated by colonial legacies.

The final weeks

At Tate, as with many cultural institutions, the few weeks leading up to the UK's first lockdown from 23 March 2020 saw a flurry of changing circumstances, hyper-speed problem solving and collapsing plans. At the end of February, we were almost confident that the Live Exhibition, scheduled for 20–29 March 2020, would go ahead – at the time, it seemed inconceivable that the spread of COVID-19 and consequential government responses would arrive so rapidly. Just 23 cases had been confirmed in the UK at the end of February, and only localised lockdowns had been introduced in China, South Korea and Italy (BBCa, 2020; Connelly, 2020; Kalia, 2020; Newey *et al.*, 2020). Nonetheless, we considered what would become the ubiquitous practice of social distancing, to ensure the safety of and provide reassurance for performers, participants, and audiences. What followed was much more drastic than what we could have anticipated and resulted in the cancellation of the exhibition and a rapidly organised recording of Linyekula's *My Body, My Archive*. To provide context of how we arrived at capturing Linyekula's performance on the eve of Tate Modern's doors closing, I will trace those changes and some of the considerations from the beginning of March 2020, drawing on my notes and emails in this first attempt to comprehend the pace and manner of the encroaching pandemic.

During the first week of March, planning and organising continued as might be expected, with some thoughts about how we might introduce social distancing where needed. From the week beginning 9 March, installation proceeded as planned and Linyekula joined us as the first, and ultimately the only, artist to perform in the Live Exhibition. This was also the week where conversations around COVID-19 shifted, and some of the participants began to pull out due to health concerns. On 12 March, however, circumstances changed dramatically. The World Health Organisation declared the COVID-19 outbreak a pandemic, and at that stage more than 125,000 people globally were infected with the virus, which had resulted in more than 4,600 deaths (Pharmaceutical Technology, 2020). In the UK, with 10 deaths and almost 600 confirmed COVID-19 cases, Prime Minister Boris Johnson stated this was the 'the worst public health crisis for a generation' (BBCb, 2020). We awoke that day to discover the US had introduced a travel ban on arrivals from Europe, and shortly afterwards Canada also advised against travel (Global Affairs Canada, 2020; Specia, 2020). It was in this context that New York-based Okwui Okpokwasili and Toronto-based Lukin Linklater had to cancel, continuing the installation by proxy with the intention to reschedule performances at a later date.

On Monday 16 March, four days before the exhibition was due to open, circumstances were changing hourly, and by the evening we were alerted to all Tate Galleries closing at the end of the following day, Tuesday 17 March. This gave us crucial time to finalise and document what we could of the cancelled Live Exhibition. Linyekula had spent much of the Monday completing his installation in the Transformers and the atmospheric treatment of the South Tank. He had worked diligently with our Lighting Designer and Consultant, Marty Langthorne, on lighting, and with his long-term collaborator Franck Moka on sound, weaving in moments of rehearsal with his other collaborators, aware that time was limited but not as drastically reduced as it was about to become. I spent much of that period consulting with Wood, working closely alongside our Producer Judith Bowdler and Linyekula's Production Coordinator, Virginie Dupray, between installation, rehearsals, and finalising the booklet for the website. Attempting to capture a sense of the moment, Wood and I added a last-minute note to the booklet, explaining that,

> this exhibition was cancelled during the escalation of the COVID-19 pandemic. As we face collective uncertainty, we are reminded of the endurance of the body through the work of these

> artists. Their work responds to the legacies of violence, isolation and fear by forging practices built on collaboration, trust and compassion.
>
> (Wood and Hong, 2020: 6)

The photographic and film documentation of the Live Exhibition now shifted to capturing what had been achieved thus far in the context of COVID-19. During the previous week, we had planned to give Linyekula and his collaborators more time to rehearse, with possible filming scheduled for Thursday 18 or Friday 19 March. This luxury of time, however, was no longer possible; with the galleries closing, and our international artist and collaborators needing to return home imminently amidst an environment of borders closing and travel disruptions. Linyekula and his collaborators – Moka, Michel Kiyombo, Ornella Mamba and Heru Shabaka-RA – only had a few hours to prepare and no time for a full dress-rehearsal by the time the performance was filmed. The significance of the recording had also shifted – it would no longer be documentation for internal purposes, but instead was to become Tate's first artistic response to the pandemic. On the day we should have opened the Live Exhibition, we instead uploaded the recording to Tate's website. It would be viewed over 15,000 times in a matter of weeks, far exceeding the numbers for a ticketed audience. The day after the performance, Wood commented that the recording of *My Body, My Archive* 'will mark this moment for posterity, beyond what the newspaper archives tell us... as art, and as collaboration' (Wood and Hong, 2020). This was echoed by Linyekula, his collaborators, and our colleagues who worked far beyond what was expected, each commenting on the personal value in capturing the performance in this time of uncertainty and the chaos we were entering. We were unaware in that moment of uploading Linyekula's performance that this was the beginning of many performances shared digitally – a reflection of how much our lives would suddenly shift online.

Recording *My Body, My Archive*

On the evening of Tuesday 17 March, a small group of colleagues who had been involved in the exhibition, and were still on site, came to the Tanks to witness Linyekula's only performance of *My Body, My Archive*. Using two cameras, the film crew, without having a full rehearsal to observe, responded to the performance in the moment and based on what descriptions we could provide. Linyekula adapted the original content for *My Body, My Archive* to reflect the context of the engulfing pandemic. As the film crew followed Linyekula and his companions through the Transformers and the Tanks Lobby, they also captured elements of Okpokwasili and Lukin Linklater's installations – a collaboration of sorts with the absent artists. During the performance, Linyekula reflects on the nature of fragility, how it enhances being alive and a sense of beauty to be found within – a concept underpinning his practice generally and magnified as we headed into the first lockdown in the UK. Moments of physical proximity and connection between Linyekula, Kiyombo, Mamba, Shabaka-RA, as well as my recollection of being in the space of the Tanks as a witness, underscore the ritual of liveness. Later Linyekula also examines the complex relationship between the body and the environment as an expansion of his concept of the circle. He explores this approach through presenting sights, sounds and critical responses to the DRC's natural environment within the performance. This chimes with Tate's commitment to address the climate emergency declared in 2019, but also seems particularly poignant in the context of the UK's lockdown experience (Tate, 2019). During the lockdowns that followed, many experienced an enhanced relationship to nature even in the UK's most urbanised environments, yet questions linger about how we will contend with the climate emergency as the pandemic's fallout continues. As Linyekula points out, all our futures are fragile, and *My Body, My Archive* offers an approach to grapple with this reality.

Throughout the performance Linyekula reveals how fragility emphasises the preciousness, precarity, and the value of being alive. Halfway through the performance, connected to his companions by a circle of light, Linyekula quotes Achille Mbembe: 'if Europe wanted to see its future, it should look to Africa because everyone's future is that of fragility and Africans have been dealing with that since forever' (*My Body, My Archive,* 2020,). As the pandemic developed, we would learn of its effects on deepening national and global inequalities, but here Linyekula emphasises different resources Africa offers in comprehending the instability of the pandemic that Europe could learn from. He continues, 'We've been dealing with the precarity of life since forever… never forget our fragility… Let's not forget that we are alive, and we are here and that is beautiful. *We are alive'* (Ibid.). It is this line which reveals fragility as fertile ground for Linyekula, echoing Taleb's antifragility, and it is the driving force behind Studios Kabako. The studio's ethos is based on art as the coping mechanism with which to face 'the enormity of the ugliness of life. To dare to dream that independence of thought, free will and personal initiative could well grow from this heap of ruins (Studios Kabako, 2021)'. This approach was made manifest in *My Body, My Archive,* not just through the words Linyekula speaks, but also in the seamless way he and his companions performed that evening. The pandemic was another fragile context within which Linyekula and his companions would find possibilities for creation.

In reviewing the recording of the performance while still experiencing remote working, social distancing and the instability of the continuing pandemic, it reminds me both of the loss of the live experience and how privileged I was to be there that night. This experience echoes how video conferencing allows us to connect virtually with others, yet underscores the physical absence of gathering in a room together. In one of the last moments of physical connection I witnessed between people before lockdown, Linyekula, Kiyombo, Mamba and Shabaka-RA create rituals of physical, visual, and sonic connection. Linyekula points out at the beginning of the performance these are as crucial for humanity as they are perilous. He explains this within the context of the pandemic, 'For such social animals as we are, it's a shock that it is suddenly the interaction with other humans that is causing this huge threat for our whole existence' (*My Body, My Archive*, 2020). While he was referring specifically to the virus transmitting from human to human across the globe, his words anticipate the damage caused to mental health, financial security and specifically, within the context of the arts and especially performance art, to the once vibrant ecosystems supporting these fields. With the lightbulb over his head resisting the darkness, Linyekula adds 'But we are here. We may not be many, gathering tonight, but wherever you are, I know there remains a certain energy between fellow humans (Ibid.)'. It is the future anterior of reviewing this recording that emphasises the significance of *liveness.* Having spent a year socially distancing from one another, watching Linyekula, Kiyombo and Mamba tenderly apply white paint with their hands on to each other's bodies seems so remote to the lockdown existence. As they write names of significant people, places and moments upon each other, the action also serves as a reminder of how our individual stories are integrated with and witnessed by others.

Yet these stories, including those of nation building and conflict, are relatively short-lived against the endurance of nature and the environment which Linyekula evokes in his performance. Linyekula presents natural habitats as both crucial to human existence/creation as well as reliant on human decisions. Linyekula elicits the DRC's rainforests and rivers through sounds and poems in *My Body, My Archive* as a continuation of his practice of relating the environment to the body and vice versa as an extension of his concept of the circle. Glimpses of video footage of his journey along the Congo River to Banataba are seen briefly near the beginning of the performance as part of Linyekula's installation in the Transformers which were also planned for projecting in the South Tank. These projections visualise Vuillard's words, spoken by Mamba in the South Tank 'Le Congo, ça n'existe pas. Il n'y a qu'un fleuve et la grande forêt (The Congo doesn't exist. There is only a river and the great forest)'. These words, spoken repeatedly throughout, question the concept of the nation in contrast to the persistence of nature, much like how Linyekula considers the knowledge of the body against the limitations of history. While Linyekula finds nature and the body to be crucial to each other's survival, he also subtly presents the instability brought by human activities. In addition to his reflections on conflict and politics, the sounds of insects, leaves rustling, and rainfall are overlayed with children laughing, and interrupted by motors rumbling. It hints at questions on what future generations will be left with as industry encroaches on the environment and a lack of political will. While the DRC's ecosystem, a reflection of global environments, has thus far outlasted colonialism, conflict and regime change, questions remain on how much longer it can continue and what effects that has on the people who rely on it. Ignoring human constructed ideas of nationhood, the pandemic and the climate emergency has ensured our awareness of our interrelatedness as we face collective threats. Linyekula brings these concerns into focus during this performance, encapsulating his symbiotic approach in the manner with which he made on the spot decisions, using the resources available and all the while reflecting and responding to the environment and the context as he performed. He evoked the DRC's rainforests and rivers in the human-constructed Tanks, contrasting their short-lived history with the deep time of nature, and the body moving in between.

Afterword

Instead of the usual post-performance celebration, a more sombre tone entered the South Tank that night. There was a collective feeling of gratitude and relief at the recording having been made, but also an anti-climax in terms of what was lost. For months, the installation of the 2020 Live Exhibition remained entombed in the Tanks during the first lockdown, uncertain of what would come next and in hopes of resurrecting our original plans. The recording of *My Body, My Archive* was distinctive to the moment in which it was created – currently, there are no plans to present the performance programme at Tate solely through recordings or livestream. Heading into the first lockdown in March 2020, many of us attempted to replicate our former lives through virtual means which may have contributed to the substantial viewership of *My Body, My Archive*. Since then, as we have settled into new socially distanced rhythms and grappled with the realities of screen-fatigue, it has confirmed Tate's Live Team's ethos that recording events is no substitute for the live experience, though a hybrid of live and livestream or recording may be the approach going forward while navigating ongoing uncertainties.

Linyekula, Dupray and his collaborators continued to create within the context of the pandemic in the DRC, releasing their video *Lettres du Congo* (Letters from the Congo) in July and later the full-length version *Lettres du Continent* (Letters from the Continent) in October 2020 (*Lettres du Congo*, 2020, and *Lettres du Continent,* 2020). Okpokwasili and Lukin Linklater also found new methods to continue their practices, navigating sonic and virtual collaborations. Many of the staff at Tate have been furloughed on and off, bracing ourselves for a future of reduced programming in a financially perilous environment, and with at least 10% of our workforce reduced and major restructuring in the organisation. We have since de-installed the exhibition, but, inspired by Linyekula's approach, we continue to look for ways to bring it back but within the radically altered circumstances in which fragility is the space we work within.

References

BBCa. (2020). China Coronavirus: Lockdown Measures Rise across Hubei Province. 23 January. Available at: www.bbc.co.uk/news/world-asia-china-51217455 [accessed 24/02/2021].

BBCb, (2020). Coronavirus: People with Fever or 'Continuous' Cough Told to Self-isolate. 12 March. Available at: www.bbc.co.uk/news/uk-51857856 [accessed 24/02/2021].

Connelly, E. A. J. (2020). First Coronavirus Death in Italy Forces 10 Towns into Lockdown. *The New York Post*. 22 February. Available at: www.nypost.com/2020/02/22/first-coronavirus-death-in-italy-forces-10-towns-into-lockdown [accessed 24/02/2021].

Global Affairs Canada. (2020). Government of Canada Advises Canadians to Avoid Non-essential Travel Abroad. *Government of Canada*. 13 March. Available at: www.canada.ca/en/global-affairs/news/2020/03/government-of-canada-advises-canadians-to-avoid-non-essential-travel-abroad.html [accessed 24/02/2021].

Harbison, I. (2020). What Does the Pandemic Mean for the Future of Performance Art? *Apollo*. 14 August. Available at: www.apollo-magazine.com/pandemic-future-performance-art/ [accessed 24/02/2021].

Kalia, S. (2020). Britain Reports Number of Coronavirus Cases Has Risen to 23. *Reuters.* 29 February. Available at: www.reuters.com/article/us-china-health-britain/britain-reports-number-of-coronavirus-cases-has-risen-to-23-idUSKBN20N0N8 [accessed 19/02/2021].

Linyekula, F. (2020). *My Body, My Archive* [video recorded performance 01:0520] *Tate.* 18 March. Available at: www.tate.org.uk/whats-on/tate-modern/exhibition/bmw-tate-live-exhibition-2020 [accessed 27/02/2021].

Linyekula, F. and Dupray, V. (2018). Faustin Linyekula – Banataba@AfricaMuseum Tervuren. *TL Magazine.* 9 December. Available at: www.tlmagazine.com/faustin-linyekula-banatabaafricamuseum-tervuren [accessed 10/02/2021].

Newey, S., Kelly-Linden, J., Harding, L., and the Global Health Security Team. (2020). Coronavirus Latest News: South Korea in Lockdown after Soar in New Cases. *The Telegraph.* 21 February. Available at: www.telegraph.co.uk/global-health/science-and-disease/coronavirus-uk-news-china-wuhan-deaths-latest [accessed 24/02/2021].

Pharmaceutical Technology. (2020). WHO Declares Covid-19 Outbreak a Pandemic. *Pharmaceutical Technology.* 12 March. Available at: www.pharmaceutical-technology.com/news/who-declares-covid-19-pandemic [accessed 24/02/2021].

Specia, M. (2020). What You Need to Know about Trump's European Travel Ban. *The New York Times.* 12 March. Available at: www.nytimes.com/2020/03/12/world/europe/trump-travel-ban-coronavirus.html [accessed 24/02/2021].

Studios Kabako. (n.d.a) *Studios Kabako.* Available at: www.kabako.org [accessed 27/02/2021].

Studios Kabako. (n.d.b) *Lubunga Monde.* Available at: www.lubunga.net [accessed 27/02/2021].

Studios Kabako. (2020). *Lettres du Congo* [video 00:23:51] *Vimeo.* 13 July. Available at: www.vimeo.com/437808307 [accessed 01/03/2021].

Studios Kabako. (2021). *Lettres du Continent* [video 01:17:54] *Vimeo.* 27 November. Available at: www.vimeo.com/484432673 [accessed 07/03/2021].

Tate. (2019). Tate Directors Declare Climate Emergency. *Tate.* 17 July. Available at: www.tate.org.uk/press/press-releases/tate-directors-declare-climate-emergency [accessed 07/03/2021].

Tate. (2020). Press Release: BMW Tate Live Exhibition: Our Bodies, Our Archives. *Tate.* 17 February. Available at: www.tate.org.uk/press/press-releases/bmw-tate-live-exhibition-our-bodies-our-archives [accessed 10/02/2021].

Taleb, N. N. (2012). *Antifragile: Things That Gain from Disorder.* New York: Random House.

Wood, C. and Hong, T. (2020). BMW Tate Live Booklet. *Tate.* 18 March. Available at: www.tate.org.uk/file/bmw-tate-live-exhibition-booklet [accessed 10/02/2021].

14 Curating community and connection in a crisis

GIFT 2020

Kate Craddock

Dr Kate Craddock is Founder and Festival Director of GIFT: Gateshead International Festival of Theatre, an annual artist-led contemporary theatre festival. Kate also works in academic contexts, currently as a Research Associate at Newcastle University. Kate was recipient of the Theatre Fellowship with the Clore Cultural Leadership Programme 2018/2019.

Gateshead International Festival of Theatre (GIFT) was one of the first festivals globally to pivot its 2020 edition 'ingeniously online' (Wyver, Guardian, 3 May 2020) in response to the COVID-19 pandemic. As many other UK festivals were postponed or cancelled, GIFT – an artist-led, annual contemporary theatre festival premised on experimentation – responded by embracing this as an opportunity to experiment further, only this time, online. While the festival format was reimagined, it was crucial that the ethos of GIFT – as a supportive space for artists to take risks – remained intact, and that GIFT's festival community could still somehow come together. This decision was made at a critical moment during the UK's first lockdown, when the experience of isolation brought about by the pandemic was relatively new, yet the desire for connection and collective experience was palpable.

During the five weeks between deciding to transition online in March and the festival taking place in early May, numerous decisions were made collectively behind the scenes, each one driven by specific challenges and questions.

As a team, we reflected on GIFT's principles, and considered how to retain our identity as a contemporary theatre festival despite the digital manifestation. We grappled with how GIFT could best support and protect the work of programmed artists in an online environment. We tested which digital platforms and formats were most suited for each event. We questioned how to build a festival community in ways akin

DOI: 10.4324/9781003165644-19

to when the festival takes place in Gateshead, a town in the Northeast of England, and which mechanisms would allow audiences to engage and connect meaningfully with one another. We sought to retain the liveness, ephemerality, intimacy, and spontaneity of how GIFT is experienced in Gateshead – where audiences can immerse themselves in the intense festival experience, and where events take place in multiple settings, many of which are non-conventional performance spaces across the town.

The following account is a personal reflection from this process that attempts to trace and unearth the strategies and approaches used to curate community and connection in a crisis.

In mid-March 2020, a few days prior to entering the first UK lockdown, I emailed all of the artists due to perform at GIFT in just over five weeks' time in sites and venues across Gateshead. I made a proposition: that in response to the pandemic, rather than postpone or cancel, we move the festival online and 'create an interactive digital experience that is in keeping with the ethos and atmosphere of GIFT' (Kate Craddock, email correspondence, 17 March, 2020). At the time of suggesting this, I had not entirely conceived what an online edition of GIFT would look like, nor how this would be achieved. I was, however, transparent with my thinking, decisions, and communication with artists, and I wanted the artists to have agency in determining how their practice might adapt.

I sent the email with some trepidation. I was already wary that we were on the cusp of there being a saturation of online performances available, and GIFT could easily get lost amongst it all. Equally, I was aware of a growing scepticism and resistance from artists working in live contexts to embrace digital modes of working. However, these felt like challenges to overcome rather than reasons not to do it.

In the conversations that followed, I was able to contextualise and frame my proposition to artists by referencing my own pre-existing creative practices experimenting with online artistic collaborations. These previous experiences rapidly became vital in this moment and gave me confidence that taking GIFT online could work.

2005–2011: Between 2005 and 2011, I spent a considerable amount of time as a theatre-maker and practice-led researcher in my role as co-director of globally dispersed performance collective *mouth to mouth*. Alongside co-director Lynnette Moran (Live Collision, Dublin) and other fellow MA Performance graduates from Goldsmiths College, London, we used the video conferencing platform Skype as a tool for creative collaboration. This became critical for us in maintaining our ensemble approach when we dispersed around the world on graduation and enabled us to create hybrid methods for performance-making. The geographical separation and attempts to remain connected via online technology became the crux of *mouth to mouth's* practice which offered a 'distinctive aesthetic involving the use of Skype technology to undercut the geographic, political and legal frontiers' which separated us (Power in Watt and Meyer-Dinkgraffe eds., 2010: 6). We embraced the Internet as a tool to rehearse and perform, and as a site for interrogation, in an attempt to maintain our connection as a collective. We created performance experiences that combined performers in studios, on stages, in galleries with live audiences, joined by members of mouth to mouth projected via Skype onto screens, bodies and objects from their kitchens and living rooms around the world. Performers were brought into the events via laptops, phones, sound recordings, postcards, and parcels. The work was highly participatory in form, encouraging dialogue and interaction between audiences and the virtual company members as we acknowledged and incorporated the fragility and failure of the technologies that we used in our attempts to remain connected. During mouth-to-mouth events, we would often invite the audience to vocally 'will us on' and help make our attempts to connect across fragile Internet connections, and geo-political borders, more tangible:

> When performers encountered a problem with technology, it was they who tackled them and discussed it openly with the audience, so that any glitches became a figure of the fragility of the technical apparatuses which support their staying connected.
>
> (Giesekam, 2007: 217)

Our experimentation with failure became core to the practice, and our work was both recognised and celebrated for this: '…at the heart of their work is a profound, humorous but often poignant, exploration of failure in performance' (Power, 2010: 6). This practice with *mouth to mouth* formed the basis of my practice-led PhD (Northumbria University, 2010) and unbeknownst to me at the time, provided crucial training for the future. It offered a model for performance that accepted (and embraced) the potential of technology failing, and strategies for how this could be carefully communicated and negotiated with an audience in real time. It produced a practice where working artistically remotely was now familiar, embodied, and where online domestic technologies were readily creatively appropriated for community building and artistic collaboration – principles that would be fundamental for GIFT 2020.

2015: GIFT is funded on a project-by-project basis. In 2015, we did not secure funding, and rather than having no presence that year, I created an online version of the festival. #TheGIFTGathering was an open access event that invited participation from artists across the world to use Facebook and Twitter as platforms for engagement and sharing materials. Many of the artists who were due to perform at GIFT in Gateshead that year took part online, sharing short videos and images as a #giftforGIFT for #TheGIFTgathering. These contributions inspired others to join in, with theatre-makers running workshops over Skype, sharing images of their practice, posting texts, songs, short films, and opening up private video links, making their performance works more widely available.

#TheGIFTGathering also operated as a crowdfunding campaign (#giftforGIFT). While relatively rudimentary in its set up and concept, it revealed a willingness and openness for theatre makers to experiment artistically online and to engage with each other's work as an audience. A festival community formed online around the event, gaining momentum over the three days of delivery as tweets and posts increased and word spread. This event came and went from timelines, with an ephemerality akin to the temporary community that comes together each year at GIFT in Gateshead. #TheGIFTGathering 2015 thus offered a framework to build upon for 2020.

2019: As part of GIFT 2019, I curated a session at Gateshead's BALTIC Centre for Contemporary Art with the title *GIFT goes Global* – an event which combined an audience in BALTIC's cinema in Gateshead with virtual contributors via the video conferencing platform, Zoom. The contributors were international artists and festival directors who were projected into the cinema for a real-time conversation with the Gateshead audience. The purpose of this event was to extend GIFT's international networks with artists and producers based in the North-East of England, and to engage GIFT's audiences with projects scheduled for GIFT 2020. At this time, Zoom was already part of my everyday pre-pandemic working life, as I was working remotely with dispersed networks of colleagues. Audience members commented on my apparent ease facilitating this hybrid space, and the event sparked curiosity, as many were not familiar with Zoom. The audience response pointed to an interest in and hunger for GIFT to embrace working this way in the future: 'Can you do more events like this next year please?' was one such request; 'maybe you could even livestream some of the GIFT performances next year to connect with some of those international festivals…' suggested another.

Little did we know what the future held.

2020: Amidst the chaos, crisis, cancellations, and the uncertainty of what lay ahead, these previous experiences combined to give me conviction and clarity. By sharing and referencing these experiences with the GIFT 2020 programmed artists, and by bringing together a core delivery team with digital expertise, we were able to instil confidence in the programmed artists in the proposed online model:

> ...we felt in the hands of some real professionals which was important for us as this was our first time to perform online...
>
> (Artist, GIFT 2020 Artist Evaluation Form)

The programmed artists unanimously confirmed that, while they had questions and concerns about what working online might mean for their practice and contributions, they were keen to be part of the festival, and to embrace the experiment. Somehow, we would work together to collectively create GIFT 2020 online.

Before planning the technical logistics, as a festival team (working remotely over Zoom) we discussed GIFT's values, and what made it distinctive, so we could better understand what we wanted to achieve in the online festival environment. We remained committed to delivering the festival within the timeframe it was planned – over three days in early May – and to hold roughly the same number of events as the original programme promised. We agreed that the events needed to remain as 'live' as possible, with multiple entry points for audiences to connect and participate. At this stage, we were not contemplating how GIFT's international reach would grow in its online manifestation to the extent it did (reaching audiences in over 50 countries), nor did we consider how many other festivals around the world would be watching us. Rather we focused on how to emulate the 'real world' version of GIFT, but in an online space. Critically, we did not conceive of this as a festival of digital art, new media, or digital performance, but as a festival of contemporary theatre and performance that embraced digital tools. By adopting liveness, connection and ephemerality as core guiding principles for the festival experience, we attempted to connect with audiences in real time as we would in Gateshead.

Core to GIFT's ethos and values have always been connection, care, dialogue, and experimentation, and we instinctively knew these needed to remain and guide the online iteration. Conversations and relationships with the programmed artists had been ongoing for extended periods of time, some over many years, and so trust had been established, which was crucial for ensuring artists felt secure in the rapid shift online.

Each programmed artist approached the adaptation of their practice to the online format differently, which enabled GIFT 2020 to manifest in multiple ways, and avoid becoming a series of streamed pre-recorded performances. Instead, we offered a plethora of options for how audiences could engage and experiment:

> …the exploration of different online platforms throughout the festival (podcasts, recorded sessions, live sessions, etc.) […] made the event feel rich and innovative, setting the way for other festival/responses to follow. I liked how there was an active consideration of forms, formats and platforms rather than simply streaming filmed shows.
>
> (Audience, GIFT 2020 Audience Evaluation Form)

Just as GIFT occurs in various non-traditional performance sites and locations across Gateshead, the online version would take place across multiple platforms and formats. GIFT events often pop up in Gateshead in surprising ways, reaching audiences who might not expect to encounter them – in the train station, by the river, on the high street, in the library foyer – and we wanted GIFT 2020 to appear to audiences with this same energy and surprise, only now the Internet was offering us our site for exploration.

One of the key considerations in discussions with artists about moving online was ensuring that we were not jeopardising their chances of performing the same works at venues and festivals in their intended live versions in the (not too distant) future. At this stage we were naively unaware how long the pandemic and lockdown conditions would last. We imagined a future when GIFT would be able to bring all the 2020 programmed artists to Gateshead to perform in person in Spring 2021, and we prioritised how best to protect, and indeed open up, future opportunities for the artists' practice. We also wanted to ensure we were protecting the artists themselves from potential mass exposure online, especially when so much of the performance material in the programme was in development, and artists were presenting online for the first time. We knew that we needed to put supportive frameworks around how works were presented, which was recognised by participating artists:

> The GIFT team were so incredibly ambitious and passionate about the artists and the work presented and managed to create a unique atmosphere that celebrated the importance of connecting with each other and the possibilities that emerge when a challenge

> (GIFT 2020 not happening in the intended way) is no longer a challenge, but an opportunity for something new, innovative and incredibly important.
>
> (Artist, GIFT 2020 Artist Evaluation Form)

We discussed placing limits on audience capacity for each event and ensured that artists who were due to present works for one audience member at a time in-person were still able to do so via Zoom. Similarly, where a performance was designed for a small, intimate audience, we capped the number of tickets made available. These were considerations that took into account the experience for both audiences and artists, creating space in the programme for distinct journeys and varied festival encounters:

> I enjoyed the variety of different platforms for presenting work, that I was able to access both with others and in my own time – I felt this was sensitive to the differing needs of audiences.
>
> (Audience, GIFT 2020 Audience Evaluation Form)

The primary rationale behind ticketing events and limiting audience capacity, as opposed to streaming all content openly, sought to protect and support artists by offering conditions in line with the scale at which they would have shown their work in Gateshead. This approach to ticketing also provided audiences with an opportunity to engage in the familiar process of booking for an event in the way they would if they had attended GIFT in Gateshead. Audience feedback gathered through our evaluation process indicated that the opportunity to book tickets was welcome and allowed people to re-connect with a sense of pre-pandemic normality. Ticketing events also allowed us to communicate with audiences in advance, detailing how they were invited to engage with each event – often with clear instructions on what device would be best for each experience, what they might need to have ready in order to participate, or whereabouts in their homes they should engage from. By building mechanisms for pre-event communication with audiences, we could establish parameters and manage expectations, and in so doing, begin to build a festival community.

The festival was ticketed on a Pay What You Decide (PWYD) donation basis, which allowed us to make the same commitment to ticketing that was planned for GIFT 2020 had it taken place in Gateshead. In the online transition, this also served to establish a sense of trust with our online audiences. The PWYD policy allowed audiences to make a donation after engaging with an event rather than purchasing a ticket in advance, which provided assurance when the reliance on technology meant there was no guarantee the event could go ahead as planned. There was a possibility that events might experience technical faults – the PWYD approach created the space for those involved to accept the possibility of failure and helped establish trust between GIFT and its audience. This strategy also pre-empted a growing sector concern around monetising online performance, a debate that continued throughout 2020.

As GIFT's move online was so firmly rooted in attempts to emulate how GIFT operates in Gateshead, the events were programmed in a way that allowed audiences the opportunity to attend every event, experiencing the programme in full should they wish. As with many festivals, when GIFT takes place in Gateshead, audiences often travel from one event to the next, and in these moments of wandering through the town together, they engage in conversations, from which a temporary festival community emerges. By programming events in real time, our online audiences were encouraged to converse and exchange with each other in between events – but this time using social media as a tool for dialogue – via a GIFT 2020 Community Facebook page, and via Twitter, using #GIFT2020. By embracing social media platforms as tools for exchange between audience members (rather than using these as platforms to share artistic content) a sense of engagement and ownership over the audience members' experience of the festival emerged. Audiences were encouraged to share images of themselves experiencing the festival, from their own homes, or from their daily (lockdown permitted) outdoor exercise. A rich tapestry of images of global audience members experiencing GIFT on their laptops, televisions, phones, in their living rooms, kitchens, cooking dinner, enjoying a glass of wine flourished across social media. This conflation of domestic and digital served to cultivate connection and community, and provide both the GIFT team and the programmed artists with a reassurance that audiences were engaging and connecting with the programme:

> There were beautiful moments and the timed and ticketed events really made me feel like I was part of the festival 'community' or sharing the gathering with others.
>
> (Audience, GIFT 2020, Audience Evaluation Form)

The majority of events took place in real time, with artists broadcasting performances live via Zoom Webinar from their own homes. The content of many of the events explicitly highlighted the complex relationship to liveness that performing under these circumstances set up. For example, in the opening speech of one of the presented works, *Elision,* created and performed by Gudrun Soley Sigurdardottir, the audience were greeted on screen by Gudrun who was 'speaking from my living room, to your living room' with a 'disclaimer' in which audiences were invited to 'imagine we are all in a room together.... sitting in your seat surrounded by each other...' (*Elision,* GIFT 2020). Moments like these across the festival illuminated the tension between the perceived immediacy and intimacy of the experience, and an increased sense of isolation and distance, bringing a heightened poignancy to the pandemic festival experience. The work was not to be experienced in isolation, but as part of a curated festival experience, with multiple opportunities for artists and audiences to come together – whether through a post-show Q&A, a party, a workshop, a panel discussion – all at a time in the pandemic when there was no opportunity to gather in person.

In the final week before the festival took place, we were in technical rehearsals with all of the artists, ensuring we were as prepared as possible for what was to come. However, it was also in the final few days prior to the festival happening that some key decisions were made about how audiences would be welcomed to the festival, and the role that I might play in this as Festival Director. These decisions were heavily influenced by my own experiences exactly one week before GIFT took place, when another festival that I had visited two years previously in Austin, Texas – Fusebox – also created an online edition. I was invited to participate in a conversation as part of Fusebox Virtual Edition, and while speaking on the panel, I was simultaneously absorbing as much information as I could from being behind the scenes, studying how the event was being realised on a technical level. I was particularly struck by the warm, welcoming tone that co-directors Ron Berry and Anna Gallagher-Ross established by making themselves part of the experience for audiences by introducing each of the virtual events. Prior to this, I had no clear plan whether I would feature as part of GIFT online, other than the panel events I was chairing, but participating in Fusebox made me realise the importance of welcoming audiences to each event, just as I do when the festival takes place in Gateshead. This act of being visible and hosting allowed me multiple opportunities across the festival to welcome and connect directly with audiences, establishing a more personal tone. In these moments, I was able to reiterate the framing of GIFT 2020 as 'a beautiful experiment', reveal the DIY nature of what we were doing, and the circumstances in which we were making it happen, which were 'unashamedly lo-fi, experimental, scratchy & inventive' (Audience, Twitter, 3 May 2020).

Additional considerations and strategies that we adopted to cultivate connection and community were focused explicitly on ease of engagement and audience immersion. We hosted a drop-in technical session for audiences prior to the festival, offering an opportunity to become familiar with the online platforms we were using, to prevent these from being a barrier to engagement. We worked with a British Sign Language interpreter across many of the events, to set a precedent and demonstrate how access requirements were a key consideration for online events – and that online does not automatically equate to accessibility. We supported artists to build tangible, shared experiences for audiences into their works, combining domestic routines and tactile material objects with the festival's digital format – at different moments, audience members were invited to eat or drink at the same time, or retrieve an object to hold in their hands while watching a performance. The programme contained multiple opportunities for conversations and participation in workshops alongside the performance works. These strategies combined to create an inclusive atmosphere around the festival, instilling a sense of virtual co-presence for audiences, at a time in the pandemic when audiences were ready for, and in need of, this. Indeed, one of the key factors behind the success of GIFT's community building was in its timing. GIFT 2020 took place at a time when terms like 'lockdown' and 'pandemic' were still a new part of our vocabulary, and 'Zoom fatigue' was yet to set in. Had the festival taken place at a different point in the pandemic, it may not have been received in the same way, or achieved the same level of connection and community.

Or maybe there was also something about our approach.

For the final event at GIFT, in a small celebratory gathering on Zoom, I offered a parting gift to the participating artists and team members on screen. With my right hand on my left shoulder, and my left hand on my right – my arms wrapped over my chest – I squeezed. A final gesture for everyone on screen who had turned up for the end of festival farewell Zoom. In our boxes of isolation, but connected through a shared gesture, as a temporary community, we squeezed, then waved goodbye.

References

Giesekam, G. (2007). *Staging the Screen: The Use of Film and Video in Theatre*. Basingstoke: Palgrave Macmillan.

Power, C. (2010). Performing to Fail: Perspectives on Failure in Performance and Philosophy. In: D. Watt and D. Meyer-Dinkgraffe, eds., *Ethical Encounters: Boundaries of Theatre, Performance and Philosophy*. Cambridge: Cambridge Scholars Publishing.

Wyver, K. (2020). Gateshead International Festival of Theatre – A Virtual, Virtuoso Delight. *The Guardian*. 3 May. Available at: https://www.theguardian.com/stage/2020/may/03/gateshead-international-festival-of-theatre-review

Postscript

Laura Bissell and Lucy Weir

The transition to online life has characterised every step of this project. Prior to our collaboration as editors, we had not met one another in person. Brought together via email by a mutual acquaintance, we had several phone conversations about our overlapping interests and our respective, embryonic research forays into the impact of COVID-19 on performance practice. As we reach the end of the process, we have still never met 'in real life' – the editing of this book has been conducted at a distance, sometimes meeting via Zoom or, more frequently, speaking over the phone. We have met only a few of our authors, who participated in an online panel event ('Performance in a Pandemic') which opened the Present Futures digital festival in February 2021. Thus, as with most creative endeavours produced during the pandemic, this book has been composed remotely, digitally, and across various geographic locations. Our intention was to capture something of this moment, in an effort to more clearly understand the impact of COVID-19 on our artforms. Yet even since the inception of this book project, the situation has evolved, adapted, collapsed, and emerged at an unprecedented rate.

As academics, we both work in environments that straddle the realms of theory and practice – a performing arts conservatoire (Laura) on the one hand, and a university encompassing an art school (Lucy) on the other. Accordingly, working across arts practice and higher education brought into sharp focus the various dilemmas facing these wider industries. We found ourselves frantically working to adapt all of our learning and teaching practices for online delivery, with very little notice or preparation time. Working for the first time in an entirely digital context led us both to reflect upon the artforms and disciplines which we research and teach, and raised significant questions about the future. What did the pandemic mean for live performance? What would performance look like after COVID? What would be lost, and

DOI: 10.4324/9781003165644-20

what might emerge? Grappling with these unknowable quandaries was challenged further by our teaching, working day-by-day with students who would graduate into an altered (some would argue profoundly damaged) industry for performing arts. This experience has been alternately humbling, inspiring, sustaining, and terrifying. Ultimately, it has revealed for us new ways of acknowledging and understanding the complex, challenging range of factors at stake for the performing arts community and its future artists during the pandemic.

These questions around the future of performance, of what was being lost and what would emerge when we could no longer work in our usual ways, were the impetus for compiling this volume. The context of quarantine and self-isolation demanded that performance change, in some ways radically, simply in order to exist. Unlike previous social or political situations that might shape the content of work, the COVID-19 pandemic has completely shifted the context, forms and mediums in which artists can work. The resulting changes to creative practices have been significant, seismic even, but it is important to acknowledge that, while some things were no longer possible, on the whole, performance-making did not stop. *Performance in a Pandemic* thus reflects the innovative ways in which artistic practices and output were adapting, responding, and evolving. As Richard Schechner observed (early in 2020, before the pandemic was declared), 'Performance Studies – as a practice, a theory, an academic discipline – is dynamic, unfinishable. Whatever it is, it wasn't exactly that before and it won't be exactly that again'. (2020: 2) Whatever the landscape of performance was before the pandemic, we will not return to that, and while much has been lost, some new approaches and hybrid artforms have emerged. An appreciation of sharing space, of venues, of the intimacy that physical proximity offers, of artforms that rely on bodies having embodied experiences has been granted, and also the possibility of making performance experiences have accessibility and diverse audiences needs at the heart of things.

There is a limit to what we can achieve with this volume, but it is an effort to capture a snapshot of a unique (and uniquely challenging) moment in time. Crucially, *Performance in a Pandemic* represents the voices of a range of disciplines and practices within contemporary performance: dance, performance, solo making, work within the criminal justice system, participatory work, theatre and live art. We acknowledge the same/different challenges that commercial theatre has also faced, but our focus has been the contemporary performance scene in Scotland, the UK, and – in this global pandemic – other parts of the world, which have been similarly and more detrimentally affected than the UK. The pandemic has revealed that we are a global community, our lives interconnected in ways we could not conceive of before. The precarity of it all – people's health, our freedom to socialise and see family, the economic elements of art-making, the gig-economy of performance practices – has been exposed to the light, made visible and seen in all its vulnerability.

We hope that this volume does not shy away from the real and often devastating effects of the pandemic on performance culture, which will be seen for years to come. As well as recording the shock of the first lockdown (in the UK mainly but not exclusively), when all looked so uncertain, we thank our authors for also demonstrating that this enforced isolation, the instruction to 'stay at home' was also provoking artists to innovate and experiment with digital platforms, for solo work, collaborations and festivals.

What happens next? What does post-pandemic performance look and feel like? With a large proportion of the population now vaccinated, the return to theatre spaces is happening. However, many artists indicate that they will also carry on with digital output alongside live work. This will no doubt be essential as we reckon with the impact of venue closures and the longer-term impact of the pandemic on the arts. Lockdowns have provoked an interrogation of what is at the heart of our performance encounters and as demonstrated through this volume, there are some key themes emerging that we imagine will continue to be explored in the coming years and months: isolation, intimacy, precarity, proximity, and perhaps, most of all, connection.

Reference

Schechner, R. (2020). *Performance Studies: An Introduction.* Fourth Edition. London: Routledge.

Index

Note: Page numbers followed by "n" denote endnotes.

For Product Safety Concerns and Information please contact our EU representative GPSR@taylorandfrancis.com
Taylor & Francis Verlag GmbH, Kaufingerstraße 24, 80331 München, Germany

www.ingramcontent.com/pod-product-compliance
Lightning Source LLC
LaVergne TN
LVHW010917110826
845149LV00013B/2393

* 9 7 8 1 0 3 2 1 9 1 4 3 0 *